The Sol Plaatje European Union
Poetry Anthology

Volume II

The Sol Plaatje European Union Poetry Anthology

Volume II

Compiled by Liesl Jobson

*The views and opinions expressed in this publication are
not necessarily those of the funder.*

First published by Jacana Media (Pty) Ltd in 2012

10 Orange Street
Sunnyside
Auckland Park 2092
South Africa
+2711 628 3200
www.jacana.co.za

© Individual authors, 2012
© Cover image: Nadine Hutton/2point8.co.za

All rights reserved.

ISBN 978-1-4314-0538-1

Cover design Maggie Davey and Shawn Paikin
Set in Ehrhardt 11/13pt
Printed by Mega Digital (Pty) Ltd., Cape Town
Job No. 001867

See a complete list of Jacana titles at www.jacana.co.za

Contents

Foreword *Liesl Jobson* xi

My grandmother breaks her hip *Saleeha Bamjee* . . . 1
Sabbath Blessing *Brett Beiles* 2
Disturbia *Michele Betty* 3
boys from seshego *Vonani Bila* 5
Sacred Passage *Vonani Bila* 12
The One Who Came First *Drees Claasen* 14
La Bourdique *Christine Coates* 15
Digby *Tanita da Silva* 16
Close *Tanita da Silva* 17
Steriele siele *Tanita da Silva* 18
Sterile souls *Tanita da Silva* 19
Uitstalling *Tanita da Silva* 20
Exhibition *Tanita da Silva* 21
The Jump *Gail Dendy* 22
The Moon Watch *Gail Dendy* 24
The day it rained in Pella *Julian de Wette* 25
Perfumed men *Graham Dukas* 27
Supermarket blues *Graham Dukas* 28
Brighton Beach *Sarah Frost* 29
The source *Sarah Frost* 30
Art Critic at the Beach *Genna Gardini* 31
The Aquasize Instructor *Genna Gardini* 33
On Words *Genna Gardini* 35

How Life Is *Dawn Garisch* 37
The Walk *Dawn Garisch* 38
Read the signs *Anthea Garman* 40
Kelp Elephant Creation *Dorian Haarhoff* 41
Shadow Speech *Dorian Haarhoff* 43
New York, 'n meditasie *Joan Hambidge* 44
New York, a meditation *Joan Hambidge* 45
Tafereel *Joan Hambidge* 46
Tableau *Joan Hambidge* 47
Tokio, 'n meditasie *Joan Hambidge* 48
Tokyo, a meditation *Joan Hambidge* 49
Mulligrubs *Kerry Hammerton* 50
The darkness of grief *Kerry Hammerton* 51
Dürer's Rhino *Geoffrey Haresnape* 53
Anthem for the old nations *Siddiq Khan* 55
Anna Frank *Kobie Korf* 61
Anne Frank *Kobie Korf* 64
Daar is iets aan April... *Kobie Korf* 67
There is something to April... *Kobie Korf* 68
'Repos Ail-bees' by Qwantani *Kobie Korf* 70
'Repos Ail Cow' by Qwantani *Kobie Korf* 71
Plaasjapie *John Kruger* 72
Country bumpkin *John Kruger* 73
Tafelberg *John Kruger* 74
Table mountain *John Kruger* 74
Aan my moeder *John Kruger* 75

To my mother *John Kruger*.....................76
Guest Room *David Maahlamela* 77
Song for Mandla Langa *David Maahlamela* 79
Whale-watching *Chris Mann* 80
Exhibit 'A' *Michelle McGrane* 82
Pipistrelle *Michelle McGrane*.....................83
Bedreigde Spesie Versus Sim-Ras *Marie Mocke* ...84
Endangered Species versus Sim Race
  Marie Mocke...................................85
Wat my tong laat loop *Marie Mocke* 86
What makes my tongue go *Marie Mocke* 87
Kgwara *Doreen Mojapelo* 88
The Burden *Doreen Mojapelo*....................90
Kapa ya ho tuma *Tsela Moloi*...................92
The Famous Cape *Tsela Moloi* 95
Kgibang banana ba Aforika *Tsela Moloi* 98
Kgibang Daughters of Africa *Tsela Moloi* 100
Remembering the Angolan Bush War *George
  Momogos*.....................................102
The syncopation of the sounds of your cowhide
  drum *George Momogos*......................104
Who are these people? *Jackie Mondi* 105
Khonani ya muduhulu wanga
  Tshifhiwa Mukwevho 107
Friend of my nephew *Tshifhiwa Mukwevho*.......107
Ndi humbela maluvha *Tshifhiwa Mukwevho* 108
Grant me flowers *Tshifhiwa Mukwevho* 108

Double-jointed Girls *Pamela Newham*	109
Third Beach, Port St Johns *Pamela Newham*	111
A Story Pretending it's a Poem *Yewande Omotoso*	112
Stranger *Yewande Omotoso*	115
The Rain *Yewande Omotoso*	116
Robberg *Marí Peté*	117
Warwick Junction *Marí Peté*	119
Four stages of surgery *Gillian Rennie*	121
Spring in New York *Gillian Rennie*	123
That Heart *Gillian Rennie*	124
The elephant is unhappy *Arja Salafranca*	125
i wish i could write *Andries Samuel*	127
Untitled *Andries Samuel*	129
Rombu Unbu *Francine Simon*	130
Tamil Familiars *Francine Simon*	131
Longitude, Latitude *Deirdre Slemon*	132
An Older Person I Know *Deirdre Slemon*	133
Things *Annette Snyckers*	135
Love strays *Abu Bakr Solomons*	137
Another Country *Tania Spencer*	138
Venice, in My Garage *Tania Spencer*	139
What will I put in my box? *Luke Stammers*	141
Bulima nigyeke *Bhekani Thabede*	143
Oh Foolishness leave me alone! *Bhekani Thabede*	145
Dlozi lami unqabe *Bhekani Thabede*	147

Just Rebuke *Bhekani Thabede*	149
Bread *Elizabeth Trew*	151
Outsider *Elizabeth Trew*	152
Raping Nation *Sandisile Tshabalala*	153
Eybers *Tobie Vermaak*	155
Eybers *Tobie Vermaak*	155
Liefdestaal *Tobie Vermaak*	156
Language of love *Tobie Vermaak*	156
Wildtuin-huisie *Tobie Vermaak*	157
Game park-hut *Tobie Vermaak*	158
Biographies	159
What is the European Union?	178

Foreword

> *The truth is a clamour, is a great rocking vibration that's brittle and sex-shelled. That's listening, a conch.*
> — Genna Gardini

What raw energy shakes the ground beneath one's feet on an ordinary morning causing nobody else to stumble? What uproar tilts the noon horizon, disturbing every upright thing, even as the rest of the world notices nothing? What is the racket that wakes one, heart racing, in the still of the night, undetected by other sleepers?

It is the forgotten dream yearning to be remembered: narrative begging space; poetry claiming form. It is her story surfacing from the underground. It is history too long denied, now yearning to be told. Those who care, stop and listen. They attune their ears with kindly curiosity and hear in the interstitial silence between clamour and vibration, the vital telltale signs of their own unspoken truth.

Sol Plaatje's multi-faceted vision included the desire to see black South Africans inserting themselves at the centre of their history. Daily, this is the task of integration for the fractured society we have become. Regardless of culture or clan, the task of restoring one's personal centre remains the work of individual consciousness and societal cohesion.

If the reader recognises the sensation that starts in the loins, radiates upwards to the heart and pulses out down the limbs, running through wrists and out at the fingertips in an irresistible urge to pen a line, then he or she knows, also, the imperative to bear witness. It starts with a word. Brings another. Yet another. In the beginning was the Word.

Recognisable by the fevered agitation accompanying the need to break free, the emerging truth pits itself against the ties that bind and spits out the gag. Whether secrets guarded by politicians, media misrepresentation or the invidious concealments inherent in corporate double-dealing, it is the unexamined story that keeps people in bondage. Arguably more pernicious than these are the hovering half-truths lurking in the individual psyche; more damaging is the self-erasure that results from censoring that which is unpalatable to oneself.

The poems included in this anthology represent a choir of voices, women and men, who listen and respond, bravely exposing the inner workings of their lives, upending their own lies. These are the contemporary shamans shining light below the surface onto those lurking elements typically veiled from awareness. The truth-tellers claim a register for the unimagined realities long shunned and denied. Their versions and visions of a more honest possibility for our society open the unthinkable and speak aloud the taboo.

Exploration and arrival, departure and return, loss and reclamation, death and transfiguration visit these pages. Grand themes and mythic archetypes, as well as miniature scenes of the daily sacredness and profanity, appear in glory and ordinariness. These are heard in strong, considered voices – occasionally loud, harsh and strident, more often subtle, nuanced and focused.

The poetry compiled from the entries received for the second EU Sol Plaatje Poetry Award represents a wider range of voices than last year. It was exciting to have been afforded the chance to select poems that speak from every corner of the country, travelogues from significant inner and outer landscapes. Exquisite tales of exploration and displacement, exile and homecoming to the body and the land have been rendered between these covers.

This year's submissions represented a stronger selection of work. It is particularly heartening to encounter a higher level of craftsmanship too. Poets are taking their work seriously. Many poems show mature attention to detail, thoughtful structure and conscientious editing. With over 200 poems to choose from, the judging committee, comprising Johann de Lange, Goodenough Mashego and myself, had a pleasant challenge to draw up a shortlist for the final judge, Oswald Mtshali.

This anthology promises to be a fascinating disruption to readers, inviting them to heed their own urgent prompts. It inspires those who come to the collection with a desire to write to join the activity, to get on with the task of transforming experience into image, incident into metaphor, and regular ordinariness into the rhythm of reclamation. This book endorses fellow travellers on the journey of poetry urging them to read more poetry, to support fellow poets and those who publish poetry. It expresses huge gratitude to the European Union for funding this vital award that enables all the voices of South Africans to emerge.

May the clamour for truth continue. May the expressive vibrations rock on. May the listening to each other never end.

Liesl Jobson
Co-ordinating Judge and Editor,
EU Sol Plaatje Poetry Award, 2012

My grandmother breaks her hip

My grandmother says we've brought her here to die.

Her paranoia probes under our fingernails
with a splintered stick,
splitting the tissue-beds, prying us apart.
We give her pills for our pain.

Her cataracts cloud over
her unlettered bewilderment.
but she can still see old blood on the ceiling
of the state hospital.

My mother is wrung, she can't sleep.
Guilt stretches out on her bed,
nesting on sheets of the unsigned hospital plan.

We've had to put a price on my grandmother.
The doctor at the private clinic tells my uncle
hip operations cost hundreds of thousands.
Old people don't make it that far.

                              SALEEHA BAMJEE

Sabbath Blessing

this lazy evolutionist
blesses the much lazier
creationists for their beliefs.

instead of slaving for millions
(or even billions) of years
to reach their present state,

they had it made in six days flat
(and some still think the earth is that)
which is why this evolutionist

gives thanks to the creationists,
for without them i would miss
this heaven-sent day of rest.

BRETT BEILES

Disturbia

In the week before
my father died,
we were gripped
by an unseen hand,
first felt in the
fleeting whine of the
eighteen wheeler that
clipped our car's side mirror
and then, in the convulsions of
a small body, as we waited on that
graveled and sandy verge,
for the child to empty
the last of her lungs
and again, omnipresent
at the edges of the lodge,
the wind whistling
in the night leaves,
with the howl and yelp of hyena
and I had shivered and wiped
the fevered brow of the child,
rinsed her in tepid water,
willing the fever to abate,
but, at the doctor's room,
I watched the doleful shake of a head
and we were ushered to the hospital
for days and drips and bad dreams,
and I remember now,
those cruel and furtive fingers,
clutching at us as we headed home,
to confront that final call –

he had tied a gnarled knot,
climbed a crooked stool
and stepped to his freedom –
and I had, instinctively,
reached for the child and
was surprised to find her
cool to the touch,
serenely sleeping,
and I sat still,
in silence.

           MICHELE BETTY

boys from seshego

you loiter through the polokwane town
knock at the door of our apartments and offices
with darting eyes
you monitor every movement of tenants
a shit job you create for yourselves
a job that only requires meanness
& the ability to ashamedly, carelessly instil fear
& fever
in your defenceless victim
with a sharp blade
& a coughing metal

you clean shaven heads from seshego
in sneakers, jeans & hats
you crawl like crabs
or just walk as if the earth is layered with eggs
you like it when the clouds brood
in streaming rains
especially in the night
wearing balaclavas & gloves
you check curtains of bedrooms & kitchens
sprinkle muthi, burn muthi
you do your job unhindered
not even dogs bark at you
no shadows follow you
& no police can trace your fingerprints
or footprints
all washed away by the rain
& dew of the night

on may day
red t-shirts clad workers
sing & dance in squares, streets & boulevards
as they celebrate the right to strike
& a living wage
but you, a merciless brigade of brazen burglars
you enter suburb after suburb
house after house
shack after shack
you shepherd the workers, your sheep
& shear their wool in this winter
you strike like slithering serpents
you search & find doors even in the dark
strike like serpents

serpents from the sprawling township of delirium,
of coughing lungs & ravaged aids frames
of cracked lipped children
crammed in the dark matchbook walls
of incestuous old aging beds
you don't sleep in winter
you roam, buzz around our dreams of hysteria
scare us with swords, pangas & guns
boys from seshego, you should be on scaffolds – rebuilding the city
you should be on farms – tilling the land
or growing crops to feed this starving nation
boys, you should be in universities sucking knowledge and skills
teaching the illiterate nation to read & write

boys, you should be on the roadside
fixing the potholes, mapping the road and bridge to mtititi
boys, you should be saving lives
that crumble like mud huts
in decaying hospitals
but here you are, scar-faced
forever drunk
dead hearts
when it's cold & dark
normal human beings fast asleep
pulling the blanket that way and this way
you break burglar doors
with crowbars and chisels
flat screens, touch screen cell phones, dvd players,
laptops, cash, clothing – your loot
sometimes you even finish of the leftover food
sell stolen goods to second-hand shops
for next to nothing
sometimes you sell it back to me
in the street
unaware

at lerato's place, apartment number 7
you took liquor from the fridge
sat on the sofas & opened beer with your teeth
& drank leisurely
then, you prepared a meal
pap, mutton & gravy
the couple and their son had locked themselves
in their bedroom

"we heard them when they came in,
we heard the noise as they ransacked
& combed the cupboards in the sitting room
we heard the noise & their drunken laughter
as the howling prowlers emptied the tv sets & jewellery box
& when my somnambulist husband woke up from his
    dreams
he pulled out an iron rod
a pepper spray in hand
i held his hand tightly:
'matome, you are not going to do silly things
these stone-hearted thieves are armed to the teeth
they'll haul & drag me like an animal
drop their pants to devour me
before they slit your throat in your pyjamas
do you want to become garbage –
a bundle of frozen worms?
you'll be lucky if these mindless wolves
leave you to stumble on crutches
please listen to me my love
you are not going to risk your life
these scumbags might put our only toddler in a bag
sell him at a baby auction
i'm too young to be a widow
to carry a void in my heart'
so the boys with river-like zigzagging scars
took what they wanted in the sitting room
then they knocked at our room
tried to open the door
we pushed back the door

screaming, help, help!
my husband with a pepper spray, trembling
we tried to call the police
but the boys vanished in the rain
before the men in uniform could come
after an hour
just three kilometres away
& all they did was take down
the statement
'so the boys didn't rape you?' they asked
& laughed at my urine wet nightgown"

april 2012: thugs with delirium were here again
here at ritruda number 12
you knew i live alone
you knew i go home to elim
you came
used crowbars to try to break in
but the bila gods held the door too tight
i only came back to finish your job
break into my house
because i needed to enter
& my neighbours who sleep in the sitting room
beside the window
just a few centimetres from my door
simply didn't hear anything
though they drink the whole night
& sleep in the morning

or they didn't want to give a statement in court
as witnesses
or perhaps they work with the prowlers from seshego
the suspects that are always at large

may 2008: burglars climbed into the roof
of president thabo mbeki's official mahlambandlopfu
    residence
in government avenue
right in the capital city, Pretoria
closed circuit television cameras watching
thieves walked away with the aluminium wire

boys from seshego, come again
come here at ritruda number 12
you'll be trapped in my apartment
run around the house which will become your anthill
swarming bees & horseflies will sting your eyes & balls
you'll not collect my double-decker bed, i bet!
you'll run around naked
dangling penises sweeping the floor
you'll bleat, slippery liquid forming from your mouths
you won't collect any red meat in the fridge
you won't take away my stove & toaster
you long fingers will be glued to my new plasma tv
because end of the month
i'm going to phafuri
that heartland of real sangomas

if need be, i'll even cross the limpopo
& mumithi river to lands yonder
sail to bileni, the land of makhayingi bila my great
    grandfather
i'll give the sangoma all my wages
we'll erect
a fence of snakes to guard my house
against you, the boys from seshego
with your souls sucked out by vampires
with the shit job you've created for yourselves
whose only qualification is cruelty

                                        VONANI BILA

Sacred Passage
For my sister, Jeannette Khensani Bila

Before the stoep of our house
Where the underground pipes lie
Khenyeza the dagga-smoking builder discovered your
    clothes
When he was diffing the foundation
I lay invisible flowers
In all seasons

I take off my shoes
Walk on this passage gently
Hold your hand, my sister
As we sip coffee together on the stoep
With our aged mother Foksia N'wa-Mahatlani Maxele

Even when the torrential rains washed away your clothes
And the remains buried beneath the ground
I shall remember that I walk on graves –
On fragile bodies of my beloved people
Whose spirits male wicked people sneeze and wobble

And whenever I discover something anew
I shall listen to your voice prickling my conscience
For every ground is covered with blood
Its pillars are human bones

As you smile Khensani, and our eyes hold each other
Know that you'll never be a *khumbi* that only remains
    behind the hut
Or buried in the wetlands of the rivers
In time, you've grown to comfort my heart
You are the holy angel
That guards and saunters in your mother's glittering
    house.

When my steps triple
And movements go astray
Carry the torch
And show me the way in darkness

What I have belongs to you
It belongs to our mother Mbati-ya-ku-fuma
Who'll soon take a warm bath of salts
And forget the pain of losing you, her last-born child
And Klaas, her first-born
And Richard, her first husband
And Risimati, her second husband

When I finally go –
I will hold your hand, again
As I join your father
and the entire Bila ancestry
emaxubini.

                                       VONANI BILA

The One Who Came First

the sky lies still
the sky lies still and it does not move
it does not move
the sky lies still
and it does not move
when it moves the sun wakes
the stars, embers of a flame, sleeps
Nkulunkulu has come again, again
the sky lies still
it does not move
it does not move
the sky

the earth moves still
the sky lies
it does not move
again, again the lizard speaks
the sky lies still
again, again Nkulunkulu
weeps the sky and it does not move

the earth moves it does not lie
the sky lies it does not weep

DREES CLAASEN

La Bourdique

The ceiling of the room is faded blue.
A large rusty hook is nailed
into the beam from which the farmer, long ago,
hung his smoked sausages and hams.
The room I am writing in is old,
outside the window pear trees
are so gnarled blossoms push
hard for spring.
Beyond them the nearest hills float
above the fog.
Early this morning, when I was still
in bed, a swallow flew into
the room, circled, saw its error,
and escaped again,
alighted on a beam
of the old barn.
Down beyond the garden is a field,
lucerne is ten inches high.
On the corner of the road, the Madonna
stands, her hands outstretched,
her veil blue.
Her back turned to me.

                              CHRISTINE COATES

Digby

Wanneer 'n reël begin bloei in 'n strofe
woord vir woord
en sonder kriewel
met net die nodigste bestanddele
van tas en klank,
gemeng met
enjambement en leesteken
uit die kern van
alle logika en gevoel
oor die positiewe, steil helling
van taal en sin
'n gladde oplossing –
hemels heilig en konsentries

Dis wanneer die sintuie een vir een, dog gelyktydig
die openbaring van 'n gedig op die hart van die siel
   ontbloot!

TANITA DA SILVA

Close

When a line starts to blossom in a verse
word for word
and without fiddling
with only the essential ingredients
of touch and sound,
mixed with
enjambement and punctuation
from the core
of all logic and feeling
on the positive, steep slope
of language and meaning
a smooth solution –
celestial sacred and concentric

That's when the senses, one by one, yet simultaneous
exposes the revelation of a poem on the heart of the soul!

TANITA DA SILVA
Translated by Johann de Lange

Steriele siele

hygend draf ek voort
op die ritme van poëtiese politiek,
soek ek mense van my eie soort
en besef telkens elke wese is uniek

Die bergie wat elke hongerpyn van sy lewe
soms kry wat hy soek, is beter af
Met ten minste iets om na te strewe
Hy sweef sweerlik salig na sy graf

uitasem hardloop ek met verwronge ambisie
en rasende roetine aan my sy
soos 'n robot op my aardse missie
al is die noodlot deel van my

TANITA DA SILVA

Sterile souls

wheezing I jog along
on the rhythm of poetic politics,
I seek my own kind of folk
and realise every creature is unique

the bergie who despite every hunger pang in his life
still finds what he seeks, is better off
with at least something to strive for
surely he floats blissfully to his grave

out of breath I run with distorted ambition
and frenzied routine at my side
like a robot on my earthly mission
even though fate is part of me

TANITA DA SILVA
Translated by Johann de Lange

Uitstalling

Soos klitsgras klou die oggend
aan my hande
Na gisteraand se
onbewerkte gedagtes,
bewolkte dialoog
en ewewydige kyke

Starend
na jou vroegnag se swart stoppels,
jou rook-gevlekte tande
tussen die walms van drank en leuens
besigtig ek jou
vir die laaste keer

TANITA DA SILVA

Exhibition

Like burdock the morning clings
to my hands
After last night's
undigested thoughts,
clouded dialogue
and parallel looks

Staring
at your early evening black stubble,
your smoke-stained teeth
between the fumes of liquor and lies
I observe you
one last time

> TANITA DA SILVA
> *Translated by Johann de Lange*

The Jump

Don't look down, he said,
but the wind was up
for the first time in days,
transforming the grass
into feathered tufts
I could run my fingers through.

I could run my fingers through
his red, tufted hair,
pull playfully on its roots
so that his head, too large
and somewhat awkward,
was brought into sight
as an orbiting satellite
on nights it seemed too hot
to breathe.
     Don't look down,
he said, and instead we'd count
the stars between the drainpipe
and the gable of the roof.

Above the gable of the roof
where the heat has blistered
both wood and paint,
the tiles appear to climb
the gradient. And so do we.
     Don't look down,

I said to my brain-damaged boy
who struggled, blue-faced,
against my grasp. He was
so very light,

almost as a bunch of feathers
in my arms. I was sure he'd fly
even as I dropped.
And the wind was up
for the first time in days.

      GAIL DENDY

The Moon Watch

When you bought me this watch
I could see everything:
the time, the date, the moon
in its different phases.

That was then. Things are different,
now. Oh yes, I can tell the time,
but the date has entered
a myopic cycle of mystery

and the moon itself is nothing more
than a shrunken orange
between painted stars
that appear only on certain weeks.

I still have the watch
and I still see everything:
the way time no longer holds you
to me, the single strand of her hair

on your jacket's lapel
like the golden second-hand
brushing across an inscrutable face.
Yes, I see it all.
This watch is unstoppable.

                        GAIL DENDY

The day it rained in Pella

In the sun-baked cathedral
the nuns sweep and dust
handmaidens marked by constant prayer.
The pulpit and altar, holiest of holies
reserved for those with clean hands
though hearts may cast long shadows
over pews.

Jesus sits under the date palms
in this place where time stands still.
Street children in tatters
a blind man babbling for a coin –
a cripple with a grizzled face
hawks oranges, the only colour here.

Jesus told the woman from Pofadder
she'd had five husbands.
She could name them all: Albi, Jukskei, Waterboer,
Kromhout, Spyker and Shaka from Karweiderskraal.
There'd never been a scarcity of men.

Her skin sallow from the sand that blows
and shrivelled like a raisin –
Lord, she asks, if you are really Lord,
why is there so very little rain?
We're tired of these blue skies.

She picked a string of dates from an overhanging palm
presented it as an offering to the Lord.
Then went back to tell the others
what the Master said.
They turned and whispered knowingly –
see what Pella has done to her.

How did the man know, how did he know
that the dates I picked would be so sweet?
And how could he tell that I would have
washed his tired feet?

But soon the tourist bus was due
and the thirsty throng
to avoid the blazing sun
and foolish talk of miracles
boarded the humble charabanc.
They missed the sight of Jesus
as He withdrew into the desert.

JULIAN DE WETTE

Perfumed men

Early Sunday morning on the corkscrew path
to the summit of Lions Head
and a mosaic of walkers
already dot the way

like the sad looking woman
drawn to the steep view,
her sadder looking feet
freed momentarily
from an inappropriate
pair of Jesus sandals.

Or the slogger dressed in nylon layers
and, unbelievably in the rising heat, a woollen hat.
What sins was he carrying to the top?

And then the oriental touring party
in their kite-coloured clothes
and their continuous camera-like voices.

But my favourite was the trio of perfumed men
whose slip-stream scent
lingered long after they'd filed up the gravel path
trailing Lentheric and Aramis in their wake
leaving me to waft down the final stretch
in my oh-so-manly way.

GRAHAM DUKAS

Supermarket blues

Had I known that our eyes would meet
sometime in the future,
I would have avoided all the salted snacks,
the last glasses of wine,
the occasional cream doughnut,
second helpings of trifle,
packets of jelly babies,
Easter eggs,
and all other waist-expanding temptations.

I would have taken up exercise,
like running or cycling or skipping or tennis,
or all four.

Instead,
I allowed my body to soften and spread.

So now, when our eyes meet
for the first and last time,
(in the aisle where the crisps
and fizzy drinks are displayed),
I know that it is too late to change course
for the sprouts, leaves and sugar-free gum.

GRAHAM DUKAS

Brighton Beach

The child walking alongside a burnished sea
turns to his mother and says 'I came from you' –
her feeling towards him a tidal rush across sand;
his truth a small waterfall, immediate as the air.

They stop, though the beach runs below a bluff
as long as the reach of the late summer sun.
Sitting in the rock pool she dips her head back into
the cold, it holds her nape, an unexpected hand.

She sees his body acute in the midday light
and remembers the girl she was; lied to, left,
a girl who heard the world beat like a mother's heart,
felt her own break over and over, like shell underfoot.

Later, in the city, the hot dark stalling his sleep,
she plays a CD of ocean sounds, pulls him into her chest.

SARAH FROST

The source

His whole life flowed like a river
from that one clear remembered pool.
The valley waterfall filled it
as fast as years passing.
He loved that farm; the land, the people.
He built cairns for it, and them –
layered a lifetime of achievements
like stones from a heartland, or fingers –
pointing to the same sky
that smiled down on him like a beautiful mother
when he was a boy, and the world was his right.

I was the daughter he would not see,
a girl hurling herself at a man half-turned away,
facing his bright future.

We visit that pool as adults, plunge bravely into
the estranged lilt of the water.
It takes my body heat
and not even the fiery sun
will give it back to me, witness, woman –
splayed out on a rock, begging, denied.

SARAH FROST

Art Critic at the Beach

This seawood is just spool.

It's green and long as a projector's tongue. And the rock it's on
seems plastic-knifed. Debowled, like an old VHS. It doesn't work for me.

But then, suddenly, the sea arrives and edits the scene out, awkwardly
washing towards, replacing. I have my suspicions about the whole thing

and scan the horizon for junior curators. And parking.

Down a ways, my girlfriend plays at the tide while I find some paper
to put this on. She kneels and welcomes the water:

I think she's sure I'm writing about her now, her body angled
so I may describe the ocean as it fleshes fresh her every part.
Is she checking if I missed that? It's no problem, she can restart.

She raises her hand to a wave, the reception of her face
    stopped,
her arm stick and familiar (she beaming "Aerial!" I
    scribbling "Mop.")
I'm fairly certain she's not noticed the condom tangling
    near her slop.

I'll wait for her to walk back.

GENNA GARDINI

The Aquasize Instructor

The Aquasize Instructor just doesn't like the look of me,
I can tell,

with my face dripping from this cap, as if twisted from a
  tap
into a shallow pool of fat

that gathers twice at the chin.
It's the gusset of ancient stockings you handmade.

I'm screwed out of my body, like a bulb.

On the first day, she berates me for not breathing
  properly:
says "If you want to look like this, you must be healthy!",

her body jerking in its costume, like biltong in a condom.

I duck down into the deep end and, snorkelling, mouth:
"I'm not this moment. I'm its document. I'll last longer!"

while old men thunder and tool towards me: sea bulls,
snapped back to movement by the water,

which does not hum and wait the way the world does,
inferring

and ushering you to death in a series of past bedrooms,
old lovers dropping from the windows like stompies.

Above, the Instructor steams and strives. Furious
as a fish in a microwave, she tells the ladies "I'm 45!"

and waits for their reactions. They pause,

then titter. They are polite. Tonight, they'll talk
to their husbands of her calves, risen and fingered

like rolls they wouldn't buy at the Woolworths.

She catches me smirking and I want to say:
"See, I'm no longer cleft like a sum by this abacus of
    bone.

I'm inking time in metres! My brain sinks two! It clicks,
then switches.

Hungry as scissors for fingers!" But she looks away.

GENNA GARDINI

On Words

She said, "Love, the only thing that lives is letters."

The truth is a clamour, is a great rocking vibration
that's brittle and sex-shelled. That's listening, a conch.

I've looked into that mouth, and asked: Did I know you
from my self's start?

From the first crustacean dollop of my brain, where both
the speaking and the tongue are still sitting, undrained?

Our lives wonder each other, disassemble like engines,
the process sudden, apparent.

Stop midspeech, take the motor out your talk.

Click the conversation from its context into a grammar
even your mother used like false teeth: a means to an end
she could take off at night. Only knowing herself when she
was just gums.

Words shamed me, so I loved them.

Laundered and spelt, I've felt each sentence as strain,
a thin membrane pulled between throat and head until
I called from the nodes of my chest, instead, humming:
Is this where I learn into myself?

Already the writing sheets above me, cursive and
 prophesying,
doing meaning mean justice, doublestitched against time.

But sometimes here,

but sometimes here you'll talk of language like a lover,
like a white-wash of water outside a church in the Karoo.

And this is how it separates you.

                              GENNA GARDINI

How Life Is

In the savoury air of the curry joint we sit
and eat – two women divorced from husbands
and lost lives. It might be the vindaloo,
or the wine, but I am crying, snot-nose,
in full view of those who wish to enjoy
their food. I'm trying to explain to you, or
to myself: how life is unmoved by who is right
or wrong, and who did what to whom; we are
mere players in a great pantomime,
performing parts which must stay true
to narrative alone; right now, this might mean
weeping salt into a chilli stew at a table near the sea –

that other consistent, unfathomed story
repeating, repeating, in the dark, endlessly.

                              DAWN GARISCH

The Walk

At first I couldn't tell where we were going.
Our conversation wandered on towards the woods,
then shied at an unexpected block. The way – so clear
when we first met – was lost for over thirty years.

We've met again. I have arrived from far
to this turbulence: two streams that habitually run alone
tumble when they converge their motive.

The sun manoeuvres low
on the wrong horizon
in this unfamiliar hemisphere;
shadows slowly arc across our path.
Brambles and ivy keep catching at our ankles.

The dogs stop
and bark
at something hidden.

You take my arm within the woods, anchor it
to yours. This warm and easy link arouses
memories of how our bodies bridged after war
when our hurting words ran stagnant.

Now we stride along, more confident,
yet still alert to that which interrupts the flow
of argument, word, heart, or even water.

We walk on, further into night, with its half-calls
and hush-flights, and creatures at the edges
staying out of sight, wanting most of all
to understand the maze that lies inside
each other's minds. We've talked

for miles through country and town,
through poetry, politics and what
went wrong. The separate lives we've lived
that fed us, now find us on this common
thrust - still not knowing how
or where we each will end,
with what pleasure, at what cost.

This time there are the dogs that roam
– and at the same time bind our walk –
snout-sniffing the track, criss-crossing
the straight, hardly ever lost. Two dogs
that know without a thought
the way that leads to home.

DAWN GARISCH

Read the signs

Is this the southern-most pool in Africa?
this slimy-floored square of
cordoned-off shallowness
in the shadow of the
         lighthouse L'Agulhas?

Screaming kids
hug the stairs
mothers in head scarves
close, but not in the water

We strip off
and stride out to the far
edge where the waves crash
and the wall is really sharp
(and the mothers watch
        us, now)

We've read the signs
        most southern this
        most southern that
We did the photograph at
the cairn: Gemma on the Indian Ocean side, me
with my feet Atlantic side

But nobody claims nothing for
        this pool

                        ANTHEA GARMAN

Kelp Elephant Creation

the beast reclines
on the beach today.
the artist offers contour
and big game shape
through patted sand,
and a washed up stump.
seaweed, shells and pebbles
embed her body.

instead of washing
at a water hole
in an inland reserve,
she graces the waves
next to the pier
with her bulk.
she's like a land whale,
this beached creature.

the sculptor shapes
her ear flaps
thin as a sting ray.
her tusks are bleached –
driftwood ivory.
he's manicured
her five toenails
in blue-bottle bubbles.

despite the sea season,
his tin trumpets
only a few coins.
tonight's tide will take
this sand mandala,
kelp trunk and all,
leaving a grey zen
loose skin of sand.

    DORIAN HAARHOFF

Shadow Speech

enroute home at last,
this everyman traveller,
Odysseus, digs a pit
in the land of the dead.
Circe, seductress, instructs
him how to call the shades.

he pours libations
round its crater rim –
milk, honey, water, wine,
barley and the blood
of a sacrificed sheep.
he settles in for a long night.

standing guard, sword drawn,
he opens his warrior ears.
clearer, more final than
wisdom from living tongues,
he listens to the ancestors
who voice their shadow truths.

                DORIAN HAARHOFF

New York, 'n meditasie

Tydens 'n slapelose nag in die stad-wat-nooit-slaap
flikker 'n advertensiebord 'n beeld van 'n stappende
   mannetjie.
Vannag onthou ek die vele mense met roet oor hul gesigte
op die Brooklyn-brug, weg van die gemaal én twee
   geboue.
Eers die werklike gebeurtenis, dan die vele voorstellings.
Uit verskillende hoeke afgeneem, weergegee en
   vermenigvuldig.
'n Vuur bly brand ter herdenking; foto's teen mure,
blomme, kruise, onderhoude met naasbestaandes, hou
die herinnering lewend: pyn is 'n slaapwandelaar
waarvoor daar geen kuur bestaan, toe of nou.
'n Polisiepet, een paar skoene en 'n speelding
uitgestal in 'n museum. Net die simboliek van skoene
maak sin: om aan te stap, beweeg, woordeloos te vlug
van hierdie sinnelose daad met geen beskerming
op daardie dag, genaamd 9/11, toe hierdie stad
vir ewig en altyd verklaar word tot ongeneesbare
   insomniak.

                                        JOAN HAMBIDGE

New York, a meditation

During a sleepless night in the city that does not sleep
a billboard flickers the image of a tiny man walking.
Tonight I remember the countless people their faces
 smeared with soot
on the Brooklyn bridge, away from the milling about and
 two towers.
First the real event, then the many representations.
Photographed from different angles, rendered and
 multiplied.
An eternal flame lit in remembrance; photos on the wall,
flowers, crucifixes, interviews with next of kin, keep
the memory alive: pain is a sleepwalker
with no cure, then or now.
A police cap, one pair of shoes and a plaything
displayed in a museum. Only the symbolism of shoes
makes sense: to keep walking, moving, to flee in silence
from this senseless deed with no protection
on that day, known as 9/11, when this city
once and for all was declared an incurable insomniac.

JOAN HAMBIDGE
Translated by Johann de Lange

Tafereel

'n Diepgroen boom
lowerryk, vol voëls wat sing,
staan in die agtertuin van 'n huisie beskeie
in Beijing. Die oompies speel mahjong,
die tantes spoel al skinderend die wasgoed,
mense fiets verby, dis skoolkomuit-tyd.
Oor hierdie klein tafereel van menslike bestaan
staan daar 'n voël opgesluit in 'n hok. Sy kraalogies
draai soos 'n arend s'n reg om dié gedoente.
Hy droom van 'n ander bestaan, 'n beter wêreld,
verby inperkings, vérvandaan, oor groot mure
veel, veel langer as sesduisend kilometer klip.
'n Toevallige besoeker sien dit alles, vou dit op
en knoop dit vas in haar geheue. So vredig
om in hierdie oomblik te wees, so ongelooflik eenmalig.

                                                JOAN HAMBIDGE

Tableau

A tree intensely green
leafy, filled with birds singing,
stands in the backyard of a modest cottage
in Beijing. The uncles play mahjong,
the aunts rinse laundrey all the while gossiping,
people cycle past, school's out.
Above this small tableau of human existence
hangs a bird locked up in a cage. His beady eyes
turn like that of a eagle taking in the hullabaloo.
He dreams of another existence, a better world,
beyond restrictions, far from there, across great walls
far, far longer than six thousand kilometres of stone.
An accidental visitor sees it all, folds it up
and commits it to memory. So peaceful
to exist in this moment, so incredibly unique.

JOAN HAMBIDGE
Translation by Johann de Lange

Tokio, 'n meditasie

'n Nokia met 'n buik gelaai vol sms'e,
'n Dell Vostro met leggers vol herinneringe
en foto's geneem met 'n digitale kamera,
twee e-posbusse wat swel by die dag.
Ek maak my los van hierdie boodskappe,
aanmanings, registrasies. You've got mail!
raas die in-boks in die Shiba Park-hotel.
Vroeër immer so 'n kamer gedeel of verlang
na die ander, die immer afwesige of vertrekkende.
Nou is die hotelkamer 'n lafenis, meer as 'n bed
in 'n stad sonder straatnommers, flitsende neon.
Ook die stad van tussenin-wees, 'n bardo dus.
Oosters, onbekend, maar wegwyser na die Weste.
En jy? Jy is reeds in San Francisco lesend aan Borges,
met 'n glas Merlot van Francis Coppola, wagtend
op 'n boodskap van my amper in die Pickwick Hotel.
Ek sal jou alles vertel van Tokio en hoe 'n gedig
Borges-agtig my gevange hou totdat jy dit lees.

JOAN HAMBIDGE

Tokyo, a meditation

A Nokia with belly loaded with SMSes,
a Dell Vostro with folders full of memories
and photos taken with a digital camera,
two e-mail post boxes bulking up by the day.
I disconnect myself from these messages,
Reminders, registrations. You've got mail!
the in-box exclaims in the Shiba Park hotel.
Earlier often shared a room or longed
for another, the ever absent one or ever departing.
Now the hotel room is a comfort, more than a bed
in a city without street numbers, flashing neon.
Also a city of the interim, a bardo thus.
Eastern, unknown, but sign post to the West.
And you? You're already in San Francisco reading Borges
with a glass of Merlot by Francis Coppola, waiting
for a message from me almost at the Pickwick Hotel.
I will tell you everything about Tokyo and how a poem
Borges-like holds me captive until you read it.

JOAN HAMBIDGE
Translated by Johann de Lange

Mulligrubs

I cultivate the mulligrubs in my
mulligrubbery, feed them night air,
forgotten desires and worms,
bathe them in leftover tears.

The mulligrubs disrupt my sleep
with their stomach cramps and
mawkish cries for water, for tea.
They invade my dreams,

with their dreams of choking
smoke and dragons, spotlights
searing their souls, rubbing
their sweaty paws along my back.

We've come to an agreement,
the mulligrubs and I, they can
visit me once a day (never
at night) and only one at a time.

They have to leave when I say.
(they don't always listen)
We've promised, on both sides,
never to step on each other's shadow.

            KERRY HAMMERTON

The darkness of grief

I imagine you already dead.

Your funeral suit flapping
around your shrunken arms and legs.
You barely take up all the room
in your coffin.

Your face jowled, your white hair
still thick,
combed forward to cover
a receding hair-line.

Today someone else
manoeuvred your feet
into your slippers,
buttoned your shirt,
tied your shoelaces,
fed you breakfast.

I imagine jets of gas,
flames hissing as they consume you.

I imagine later that night
those of us left behind will dowse each other
for memories

to fade the darkness
of our grief,
and bicker
about where to scatter your ashes.

KERRY HAMMERTON

Dürer's Rhino

These days I've turned from oils and silverpoint
to work as *reisser*, woodcut man.
Propelling gouge or chisel,
I set that hump upon you
re-inforced with nervy tendrils.
Your massive head
is sloped towards the earth,
a ploughshare set to open up the tilth.

Across your flanks, fat thighs and shoulders
I fix in armour plates –
tap, tap – with rows of rivets.
Your four squat legs – pilaster-like – are scaley
and, all along the skirting of each foot,
I plaster in your claws like tiles.

Not known in Europe for a thousand years,
you lunged into the Lusitanian ring
[making a rumpus, matching horn to tusk]
to drive away the uptight elephant.
The Elder Pliny's narrative
was proven true.

I make you my testudo,
age-old tortoise,
ponderous upon the battlefield.
Your straight and tasselled tail
thrusts down and outward
like a legionary's spear.

The frill beneath your throat's
a grim crusader's gorget.
Somewhere behind
the funny funnels of your ears
I've given you a second spike
that's supernumerary.

You are my burly beast – all immanence,
infallibly *here*, a fleshly miracle,
playing out a passion in the biosphere.
Your provenance is scriptural.
Behemoth and Leviathan
applaud you from the gallery.

Curved by my narrow knife,
your lips are grasping on a fuzz of provender.
Perhaps the *spiel* in German,
a date, your Latin appellation, and my monogram
are not the only tabs I have upon you.
Is that the eye of Albert
peering
through the peephole
in your carapace?

       GEOFFREY HARESNAPE

Anthem for the old nations

'The dominance of the Dutch-speaking Bastards in the area is left in no doubt.'
— Anthony Traill; *The rush of the storm:
the linguistic death of /Xam*

Part One

Now, Muses, let us begin to sing of younger men...

Not only then, in that gap between
vanishing from sight like slow-ringing vision
right behind the camera-flash.
Not only when, swollen

in one damp gash or another
of granite folds eroded by millennia.
Slowly, bouncing off a lonely koppie at any
moment, lapping at a wharf, whistling over a freeway

faint, buried by the static of successive generations:
a thing that falters through the wind then sinks.

*Only love is ours.
Only love is
ours. Only
love is ours.*

You'll hear it. A buffeted stone
blown to bits, that slowly showers home.

Part Two

And the rain did thus, the rain seemed to shine into our eyes, and the rain, as we were thinking, that the rain was going to lighten, and it seemed as if the rain closed our eyes, when the light was in our eyes. We stared shutting our eyes, while we felt that, it was as if it were darkness which kept our eyes closed. And the rain while we had not yet opened our eyes, the rain gave us things which our eyes were as if they were green, on account of them; and the rain lightened… while our eyes were as if they were green and the rain lightning went over us; and the rain… a stone which stood outside in front of our home, the rain lightning struck it, and my mother exclaimed; my father questioned my mother, as to what was the matter with her. Had the rush of the lightening reached her, that she exclaimed as if in pain? And my mother said to my father about it, that, the thing seemed as if the lightning were tearing off her skin.

– after the 19th Century /Xam of Dai!kwain's
The Thunderstorm

Part Three

How many times you walked up and down there,
that narrow barren strip down at the tip
of the continent, nobody could say.
The docks built block by block by jailed bushmen;
the fat, content, incontinent streets, shop
on shop; the flaccid pavements of which they
formed "the still centre of the turning sphere".
You would never bother to count. Whether
from indifference or fear of the answer
there was never a step could count for shit
except the next one, the one that would come
and finally fling you the hell out of here.

That night you were on the prowl for people.
Careless of the empty stretches between
clubs you wandered to the watering-hole
of the east, and then to the west. Nothing.
Cops patrolled the roads. Taxis prayed for prey.
There were no people. The petrol station
next to the gay-bar appeared to function –
there were lights, there was noise and transaction –
but in the movement of all these objects
and their prices there was clearly no-one
there, where world whirred into word, waned
into blurred which whirled wayward into here.
You stood and stared at the shopping-centre.

This building, built in 1848* –
nothing but a face,
the hair of a hundred and fifty years
towered above it.
Empty stress trussed-up, nothing but a farce
towered above it, a head traced
with whipped-up tresses beat hard by the force
of a sedentary, elementary herd.
Rock-façade, sedimentary air-head,
glass teeth bared in smile, snarl, gnarl or grimace.

Steel brain strained towards heaven – it spoke
of still borne progress, of opulence stone broke.

Part Four

"I lived in those times. For a thousand years I have been dead. Not fallen, but hunted…You who live, what have you made of your luck?"
— Robert Desnos; *Epitaph*

Reader, so many of us have gone before.
So many more are still to come. Paper,
clay tablet, cave wall or liquid-crystal display:
there's little difference between the stories they tell.

The rush of the storm
seems slower than the wind from a cannonball;
the bomb-blast blares louder than the call of thunder.

Our ears pick out some order
in the attack each noise scrapes into the air
but fail to track the duration.

The trail grows cold. The orchestration
obscure. What remains are "The immortal
hydrocarbons of flesh and stone:

'Here, the impressions in this fossil
indicate the movement of one
person to another.'" Because I moved,
I came to know her. Because I knew, I loved.

I'm not Buddah or Baudelaire
but I'm just as good as they are
because I will be remembered
for nothing but my love of her.

Recapitululation

Grandfather,
a voice I am going to send.
Hear me!
All across the universe,

a voice I am going to send.
Hear me,
Grandfather.
I will live.
I have said it.

> – after the 20th Century Teton-Sioux of Red Bird*'s*
> *Opening prayer of the Sun Dance*

SIDDIQ KHAN

Anna Frank
Ryntoer 2009

Liewe Anna
Ek het vandag jul achterhuis besoek
en saam met jou uitgekyk op 'n troostelose
dag en troostelose omstandigheid.

Jul uitgerekte ontberinge is onvergeeflik,
onvergeetlik. Amsterdam was nie die grote stad
vir jou, maar grote angs, ingeperk tot jul klein
leefruimte, elke dag so steil soos die trappe na jul
wegkruiplek daar bo.

Die Duitsers immer aan't marsjeer
soos bloedhonde in die strate
wat sou 'n Jood se sonde so groot maak
dat hy nie meer 'n mens durf wees?
Sy beendere opmekaar gegooi
'n laaste wanhoops-omhelsing
as die lewe niks word by Auschwitz se dodedans

Jy moes buite wees met jou vriende
op jul fietse deur die strate
al bekommernis die om 'n oulike kêrel se hart te steel
'n puisie op jou wang
of wat om aan te trek om hom te vang

Die hoop het bly vlam dat
die wrede oorlog sou eindig
dat julle die deur kon oopgooi –
die trappe afstorm
die lewe kon aangryp

Wie kon so verraderlik wees –
wat was die wins…
jul skuiling verklap,
die barbaarse stewels wat in jou siel sou trap
weereens 'n gevangene
wreder, erger, geskei van mekaar…
niks om voor te leef

Nie eens meer jou vertroueling die
rooi dagboek; jou bondgenoot
"met schrijven word ik alles kwijt
m'n verdriet verdwijn, mijn moed herleef."

jy wou vry wees van die haatlike
verdrukking die lyding die seer –
tot jou broosheid verkrummel
jou tenger liggaampie agterlaat
om vir ewig vry te mag gaan.

Uit alle wêrelde kom mense saamgedrom
by Prinsengracht 263
en deur die leë vertrekke
word mense se harte volgemaak met emosie

Anna ons sou jou nooit verraai,
maar dit het hulle ook vir die Meester gesê –
en omgedraai en Hom gesoen

Doen jy ook aan by soveel lande
as waarvan mense hier kom besoek?
Het jy al by die suidpunt van Afrika se son kom
baai waar julle Jan van Riebeeck
vir ons 'n vasmeer plek kom maak

Jou pa sê hy het nie jou binnekamer geken
dat hy nie jou diepste gedagtes kon raai,
Geen mens is 'n eiland
sal ons dit van julle leer
om oop te maak,'n brief vir jou geliefdes te
wees want waar eilande saamkom
vorm 'n hegte kontinent

Nou weet ons, laat almal wees wat hulle wil –
Engels, Duits, Nederlands of Afrikaans.
Hoe kon iemand sy herkoms kies…
solank ons elkeen sy menswees gun
dit is tog net deur ander dat jy self mens kan wees
Ons eer jou Anna
jou moed
jou durf – jou INSPIRASIE

                                  KOBIE KORF

Anne Frank
Rhine tour 2009

Dear Anne
I visited your achterhuis today
and with you looked out on a bleak
day and dismal circumstance.

Your drawn out hardships are unforgiveable,
impossible to forget. Amsterdam was not the big city
for you, but immense fear, restricted to your small
living quarters, every day as steep as the steps to your
hiding place up there.

The Germans always marching
like bloodhounds in the streets
what could've made a Jew's sin so big
that he ceases to be human?
His bones thrown in a heap
a last desperate embrace
when life comes to naught at Auschwitz's funeral dance.

You should've been outside with friends
cycling through the streets
the only worry how to steal a cute guy's heart
a pimple on your cheek
or what to wear to catch his eye.

Hope still a flickering flame
that the cruel war would end
that you could throw open the door –
storm down the stairs
and grasp life.

Who could be so treacherous –
and to what gain…
betraying your sheltering place,
the savage boots trampling your soul
once more a prisoner
crueler, worse, separated from one another…
nothing left to live for

Not even your confidant
the red diary; your accomplice
"met schrijven word ik alles kwijt
m'n verdriet verdwijn, mijn moed herleef."

You wanted to be free of the hateful
oppression the suffering the hurt –
until your frailty crumbled
leaving behind your brittle body
to go free forever.

From all across the world people gathered
at Prinsengracht 263
and the empty rooms
filled the hearts of everyone with emotion

Anne we would never have betrayed you,
but one said that to Jesus too –
yet turned around and kissed Him

Have you also visited as many countries
as have visited you here?
Have you bathed at the southern end in Africa's sun
where Jan van Riebeeck
created a safe haven for us

Your father said he never knew your inner room
that he could never guess your deepest thoughts
No man is an island
is the lesson we learned from you
to open up, to be a letter to your loved ones
because where islands meet
a secure continent is formed

Now we know, let everyone be what they want to be –
British, German, Dutch or Afrikaans.
Nobody chooses their origin…
As long as we grant each his humanity
it is through others that we can be fully human
We honour you, Anne
your courage
your daring – your INSPIRATION

KOBIE KORF
Translated by Johann de Lange

Daar is iets aan April…

Daar is iets aan April wat op jou kom lê soos perskereën –
'n gul portaal van 'n lang mooi somer wat was.
April is vir oulaas… en ver verlang
'n lepellê van seisoene, van afskeid en vertrek
April is blertse lou sonkolle in my Bulwerpark oraloor
'n Pierneefboom wat opreik in fyn, dun vertakking,
'n kiepersol wat uitwaaier oor al die somer se onthou

April is 'n uitspattige palet van herfs, kleure wat oopbars in
'n Josefskombers van blare – oker, ougoud, roes, olyf, pruim.
April is die inspit van somer, bestek neem, 'n belofte van 'n weerbegin.
April is dae van sy, soel aande met 'n speelse byt

Daar is iets aan April – 'n najaarstruitjie wat om jou skouers vou.
April is guitig, verleidelik, 'n wulpse skoorsoek teen die winter,
'n nostalgiese vashou aan 'n beleë somer.
April is verootmoed, 'n gebed van vernuwing 'n afgaan op jou knieë,
'n rypword van genade…
April is Pase
April is so April

KOBIE KORF

There is something to April…

There is something to April that settles on one like peach
    rain –
a generous porch of a long beautiful summer that was.
April is for the last time… and far off longing
seasons spooning, farewell and departure
April is splashes of tepid spots of sun in my Bulwer park
    all over
a Pierneef-tree reaching up in delicate, thin branching,
an umbrella tree fanning out over all of summer's
    remembrance

April is an extragavant palette of autumn, colours bursting
    open in
a Joseph's blanket of leaves – ochre, old gold, rust, olive,
    plum.
April is the digging in of summer, surveying, the promise
    of a fresh start.
April is days of silk, sultry evenings with a playful nip

There is something to April – an autumn-sweater around
   your shoulders.
April is playful, seductive, a wanton banter with winter,
a nostalgic clinging to a mature summer.
April is humility, a prayer for renewal, going down on
   one's knees,
a maturing of mercy…
April is Easter
April is so April

KOBIE KORF
Translated by Johann de Lange

'Repos Ail-bees' by Qwantani
Met verskoning aan Totius (Repos Ailleurs)

Sy staan bonkig, stewig, gepantser in haar sterk vel
Jy is so onverstoord, gelate, tevree
Weet jy van die vinnige eeu
Die stress wat jou van binne vreet
Kon ek so rustig tussen julle wei in
volkome simbiose –
Bolle gras inwerk en lig verpak, later saam afhurk in
vriendelike kring en in herkou die dag saam te oënskou.

Sy staan weeïg teen die heining aan die pad
sielsoë turend in die grou, sou die
weer verbytrek, sal dalk moet aanstoot
om 'n honger pens te vul.
Kyk die blink gevaarte, so vinnig, droogvoets
oor die klipperpad
Sou weelderig in dié affêre kon teruglê teen sagte leer
in sy knus beskutting en agter slierte reën aan vinnig
beter weiveld op kon spoor.

KOBIE KORF

'Repos Ail Cow' by Qwantani
With apology to Totius (Repos Ailleurs)

She stands chunky, sturdy, armoured in her strong skin
You are so unperturbed, resigned, content
Do you know about the rapid century
The stress eating you from inside
If only I could graze amongst you in
perfect symbiosis –
Working in tufts of grass then lightly packed, later
    crouch in
a cozy circle and together ruminate the day taking stock.

She stands feeling faint against the fence along the road
soulful eyes staring into the grey, should the
weather pass, maybe should get moving
to fill a hungry stomach.
See the shiny colossus, so quick, high and dry
over the gravel road
Could've reclined luxuriously against the soft leather
in its cozy protection and behind streaks of rain rapidly
have tracked down better pastures.

KOBIE KORF
Translated by Johann de Lange

Plaasjapie

Die dreungeluid van wiele op die teer
maak my ore seer.
Blikgevaartes skarrel heen en weer
en maak my ore seer.
Waar is die stilte op die plaas?
Wanneer laas
kon ek die skor geskree
van korhane teen die randjie hoor?
Wanneer laas
het die sewe-ster
glad nie ver
bo my kop gehang?
Ek is vasgevang
In 'n mengelmoes van stadsrumoer
Eendag sal ek graag weer
Op die plaas wil boer…

                    JOHN KRUGER

Country bumpkin

The roaring sound of tyres on asphalt
hurts my ears.
Metal monsters scurry to and fro
and hurt my ears.
Where is the silence of the farm?
When last
could I hear the hoarse call
of heath-cocks from the ridge?
When last
did the Pleiades
hang above my head
not that far away at all?
I'm caught up
in the jumble of city noise.
Some day I'd like to
farm once more…

                    JOHN KRUGER
           Translated by Johann de Lange

Tafelberg

Tafelberg staan vanmôre grys teen blou
Hy staan en wag vir my en jou....
Onthou jy nog die stad se liggies
en al my kort gediggies?
Ons het teen die berg se hang
'n stukkie HEMEL vasgevang.
Ou Tafelberg staan steeds grys en blou
en wag vir my en jou....

JOHN KRUGER

Table mountain

Table mountain this morning stands gray against blue
He waits for me and you...
Do you remember the city lights
and all my short poems?
Against the mountain slope
we caught a piece of HEAVEN.
Old Table mountain still stands gray and blue
waiting for me and you...

JOHN KRUGER
Translation by Johann de Lange

Aan my moeder

Ek wil vir jou
Bosse blomme bring,
Ek wil vir jou
My mooiste liedjie sing…
Ek wil 'n wolkekleed
Vir jou vind
Reënboogkleure om jou bind.
Ek wil wag onder by die kaai
Wag tot die suidooster
Jou na my toe waai…
Ek wil jou styf vashou
Tot die maan
Op sy baan
Stil gaan staan…
Ek wil…
My wil is tevergeefs, te laat
Ma het ons lankal reeds verlaat…

JOHN KRUGER

To my mother

I want to bring you
Bunches of flowers,
I want to sing you
My most beautiful song…
I want to find you
A cloudy dress
Around you rainbow colours bind.
I want to wait down below by the quay
Wait until the southeaster
Blows you to me free…
I want to hold you tight
Until the moon
Stops moving
On its way…
I want…
My wish is all in vain, too slow
Mom has left us long ago…

JOHN KRUGER
Translation by Johann de Lange

Guest Room

I slept at the guest room
each night she hosted me
in her uncluttered uptown apartment,
the intension was transparent:
I wanted to be more than a guest.

Our lips often collided randomly,
at times we found hands beyond barricades
yet we both knew
she is a stainless-steel woman of principles,
a not-lonely loner who audits her sensuality.

No woman ever lionized me
with soulfully-cooked food like her,
I always relished her tasty meals,
but deep within, my heart whispered:
you would relish her infatuation even more.

We did what we did not do,
or you could say
we did not do what we did,
I enjoyed her prelude chivalrously
as she slowly opened curtains to her heart.

Like a hibernating serpent
situations pushed me to disrobe the old me,
I evacuated her ascetic theatre
before the beginning of the episode,
left her performing without audience.

I'm not sure if she loved me
out of passion or compassion,
as she once declared
that there is no spark between us
and nothing will ever be.

Though I'm at harmony with the hermit I became,
I miss waking up at her guest room
not bothering about preparing the bed,
she always prepared it her way even after I did,
like hotel attendants do when you try to impress them.

DAVID MAAHLAMELA

Song for Mandla Langa

I have heard many songs in my life
songs that perished as soon as they knocked
but yours forever echoes in me,
song that defeated grinding teeth of time;
songbirds are caged in the freedom of their open nests,
they do not hunt for food anymore,
someone is feeding them from there,
their sweet chirping melody does not go beyond the nest,
they no longer speak to us in song.

They sold their beaks for gold,
they are ghost writers of tunes in political speeches,
speeches that declares the cutting of trees that house their
    nests,
they can no longer warble for themselves without beaks,
what they master is to write what they cannot read,
but all is perfect in their warm restful nests,
as long as they are not exposed to the baleful outside,
hence someone is feeding them from their nests,
they no longer speak to us in song.

DAVID MAAHLAMELA

Whale-watching

I was standing in a hot bright wind on a headland
looking out across the sea with a pair of binoculars
when I heard a voice call out, 'Look, there they are!'

My wife was pointing, she is in a way still pointing
across the crowds and the sun-umbrellas on a beach,
the lifeguards on a stand, the tiny heads in the waves.

I swung the glasses and saw a trough of rough water,
breaking, sealing, lifting and dropping in the swells
just where the edge of the land falls like a precipice.

'But isn't that a reef?' I asked. 'Or dolphins, playing?'
I gave her the binoculars. She put them to her eyes,
fiddled with the focus-wheel then stared and stared.

'No, it's them alright!' she said. 'Next to the gulls,
a mother and calf, I can even see the white patches,
what are they, like warts, along the top of her head!'

She handed me the binoculars. I paused, uncertain.
A spurt of gloom, as dark as the ink of an octopus,
was billowing through what little I knew about whales.

I'd seen Captain Ahab again, standing in a longboat,
gripping the tiller in the stern, stump-legged, cursing,
goading on the rowers, an eyeglass pressed to one eye.

What did he see in that brass-cased deadlight of a lens,
a blubber-hulk, breaching a swell like a whale-oil tank?
A devilish dark malevolence, tail up, spoiling for a duel?
Or did he foresee a kill, the dark-grey, heaving mound
roped to a ship as men in spiked boots sliced at its back
and gulls screamed and off-cuts floated on a slick of gore?

Enough of that, I thought, *no more of Ahab's nemesis,
at least for now!* With that I shook him off,
I shook old Ahab's muttering ghost right out of sight

and saw in the bright glass portal of the binoculars
a whale-song mother wallowing with her calf
across the light green swells, the white sand of a nursery.

Rising, sinking, sieving the water with mouths agape,
shooting up breath like towers of bubbled, airy light
they swam protected seas, safe in that open-ended O

the halo of a saving vision, a vision which had made,
at least for now, the blood-dark seas of Ahab's line
a salt-bright sanctum for the song-ships of the deep.

CHRIS MANN

Exhibit 'A'

The McGillivray barn
before the family murders:
To the right you can make out
the timbered stalls, the chaff
scattered across the stone floor
and at the far end
the open double doors;

then, you may notice
the recycled iron hooks hammered
into the central crossbeam.
Six of them, newly installed
by the blacksmith who carried out
the instruction insisting
with a shake of his head
they were mounted too high
for halters and bridles.

You won't hear the children's
laughter as they clamber over
the combine harvester in the yard
or see Sissy McGillivray, framed
in the kitchen door on baking day,
wipe her hands on her apron,
call them in for lemonade.

        MICHELLE MCGRANE

Pipistrelle

He had forgotten how to walk,
the child they found roosting
upside down in the cave depths,
cauled in silence and darkness,
arms folded across his chest.

For years he had gleaned beetles
from the chamber floor, snaffled
moths and mosquitoes in mid-air,
lapped from the silted pool at twilight.

Startled by halogen beams,
spelunkers' thudding boots,
his family, roused from torpor,
had abandoned its crevices, swarmed
above the harnessed men,
through the hibernaculum mouth
and disappeared into the woods.

Now, monitored by behaviourists
behind an observation pane,
the boy huddles on a cot, his head
against his knees, eyes closed,
squeaking as if echolocation
might guide him home.

MICHELLE MCGRANE

Bedreigde Spesie Versus Sim-Ras

posbus is bedreigde spesie
posseël is bedreigde spesie
handskrif is bedreigde spesie

tyd vir troetelbande ly aan
kuber-rotgehol en selfoon-
oorbevolking wat met afskeep-

kitstaal alle ratte van kits-
geld-laat-rol en tydsny toets,
sms in plaas van brief skep

brief – die hand *au fait* met warm
vrywe oor papier, omarm
eensames wagtend op die posbus...

briewe het helaas gesneuwel
met die kudde knap met duimnael
knap met kodes – dis die knapknip

    nuwe sim-ras

piep-piep – *MESSAGE READ* – *eks ok*
wane ko jy + *hu gan it*
duim *delete... delete*: wis uit

        MARIE MOCKE

Endangered Species versus Sim Race

post box is endangered species
postage stamp is endangered species
handwriting is endangered species

time for pamper-bonds suffers from
cyber-rat race and cell phone
overpopulation with skimpy

txt lingo turning the cogs making auto-
money roll and testing time slicing,
sms instead of letter writing

letter – the hand *au fait* with warmly
rubbing paper, embrace
lonely hearts waiting at the post box…

letters alas perished
with the herd smart with thumb nail
smart with codes – the smart card

   new sim-race

peep-peep – *MESSAGE READ* – *im ok*
whn ru cmng + hw r u
thumb *delete… delete*: rub out

                       MARIE MOCKE
               Translated by Johann de Lange

Wat my tong laat loop

my wetenskap?
'n potlood
wat sprinkane en syfers verslind

my wetenskap –
blou bosoë
wat plaashekke oopstoot

my wetenskap,
'n doringbos
benede my wat swere oopsteek

my wetenskap,
pentatol
wat gal by Lethe uittap

my wetenskap!
sterre sewejaartjies
wat my tong laat loop

                MARIE MOCKE

What makes my tongue go

my science?
a pencil
devouring locusts and numbers

my science –
blue bush-eyes
pushing open farm gates

my science,
a thornbush
underneath me lancing ulcers

my science,
pentathol
drawing bile off Lethe

my science!
stars immortelles
making my tongue go

                    MARIE MOCKE
Translated by Johann de Lange

Kgwara

Tetšwana tša go balega o khukhušitše,
Lesoganamantsatsarapana lelekelekgwathalegodimo,
Wa ipona o le monna o ipheditše,
Katara ka lapeng leno ya letšwa ke wena,
Batswadi wa ba bintšha ka dinanantlhana seretseng,
La gago ya ba la kgoši la go agelwa legora,
Wa ba buša ka ya tšhipi lapeng la bona.

Tšatši la hlaba re tsošwa ke wena,
Ge o nyaka ya go reka sekala o ba mogogonope,
Ka mahube a banna o šetše o hlabile lešata,
O re hlodia bokanose e boka tsebeng,
Mašeleng a mphiwafela ge a sešo a fela,
Batswadi ba ka se bo pate boroko,
O kgaritlela ka moka le sente ya mafelelo.

Etse o a gopola gore mengwaga e namela thaba?
Thaka di fata di fatile mafate a kgwale,
Wena o buna ka sešegong sa batswadi
Tše nkego tšhemo ke sebata e louditše meno.
Afa o a lemoga gore kota e llwe ke mohlwa?
Ramasedi a ka no ba gopola,
A ba khutšiša komamotšhaotšhele mailagoaloga.

Ge tetšwana tše di go botša gore o monna;
Sa monna ke go atha jase ge letšatši le hlabile
A tseba go sela le bangwe banna,
Ge e le sego sa meetse a goroša, lapa a ikagela la gagwe,
Ya ba gona sehlako go lla sa gagwe.
Tlogela go re hlokiša khutšo, kgwara towe!
Ga se rena re rilego o be mathinyane mailathuto.

                DOREEN MOJAPELO

The Burden

You have grown a few facial hairs,
The tallest guy who can touch the sky,
You see yourself as a complete man,
You play your own guitar and expect everyone to dance
    to it,
As for the parents you are dragging them in the mud,
And your voice is the king's, it must be obeyed,
And you rule them with an iron hand in their own house.

In sunrise we are awakened by you,
When you want money for booze you act like a rooster,
At dawn, you make a lot of noise,
You irritate us like a bee in our ears,
When the pension grant is not yet finished –
Your parents know no sleep,
You take it all until the last cent.

Do you realise that the years are multiplying?
Your peers are doing it for themselves outside,
You are busy draining your parents' savings,
As if you will die if you can find a job.
Do you realise that they are ageing?
The Almighty might remember them,
And relieve them from the never-ending initiation.

If your silly goatee tells you that you are a man,
Then a man's responsibility is to wake up when the sun
 rises,
And fend for himself together with other men,
And find a soul mate and build a home,
That will be when his rules will be obeyed.

Stop giving us grief you troublesome one,
We are not the ones who said you should hate school.

DOREEN MOJAPELO
Translated by Mpho Molapo

Kapa ya ho tuma

Kapa ya ho tuma.
Kapa ya maobane le kajeno.
Kapa ya dillo le di tsikitlano tsa meno.
Kapa ya botle le monate hoba bang.
O mpakela mahlomola ha ke nahana ka wena.
O mabitso bitso a melata.
Wena ya hlokang mabitso a bana bathari e ntsho.

Ba kgothuba baleleri hodima hao,
Ba theosa ba nyoloha ka bophara ba hao.
Ba nwele metsi a hao ba kgolwa.
Ba jele di chekwa tsa hao bafola.
Empa ha e le lebitsonyana la hona.
Ke wena Kapa ya ho tuma.
Dithaba tsa hao di bitswa ka bo Tafole, hobaneng?
Le lefeng la ba Bakgothu, banga ba naha?
Ha o le Kapa tjena, ebe ka Sekgothu o mang?

Kapa ha wa tuma feela ebile o botle bona ba dihole.
O engwe ya dinaha tse ba batsehang lefatsheng.
Ha se fela baile ba fihla mme, ha baka ba hlola ba kgutlela morao.
O seema hale sa sekgutlong sa entsho kontinente.
O moo mawatlehadi a kopanelang teng.
O moo baneng ba rongwe basa ka ba fetela pele.
Jo! nna le ha sekepe se ile sa robeha,
Ha le ya se lokisa keng mme la fetela pele?
Le kwana India ha e sa le ba le emetse.
Ha e sale Lanselara le le emetse hore le kgutle.
Hobaneng baile ba phahamisa mahlo a bona?

Nkabe baile ba lokisa dikepe ba ntse ba toname.
Ba sa bone botle banaha ya bana ba Bakgothu.
Ba se bone le yona Thaba e kareng ke Tafole.

Ba hana ho ultwa monate wa merohoya naha.
Ba hana ho bona dikgomo tsa Bakgothu tse nonneng.
Le mahlo ha a ka a tloha le ho basadi ba naha.
Bao baneng ba le basehlana ba le dikoti marameng.
Le Lekanselara le ile la makala ha masowa a sa kgutli.
Le ile la nyala la ba la tempa.
La nyala baradi ba Rantsho,
Empa kgethollo ya mmala le tswa hole le yona.
Le ile la kolobetswa ka yona ka sebele.
Kgethollo ya mmala ha se ngwana wa 1948.
Ha e sale lefihla ka yona mohlang le fihla kontinenteng e na.

Ebe basadi ba dikafore le ne le ba kene kene eng?
Hobane lona le bana ba bao ba kgethilweng.
Le tswetswe pele ebile le bo re ya tseba.
Empa dithope tsa naha diile tsa le kopanya dihlooho.
Jo! Nna le e ahile Kapa jealous down!
Le e lokisitse ya tshwana le Holante, mose ho mawatle.
Ebe e ahilwe ka madi le mofufutso wa bo mang?

O ka e fumana o le Kapa ya ho tuma ware ha o mona
 Aforika!
O ka nahana hore ke engwe ya naha tse mose ho mawatle.
Meaho ho kopiwe ya mose,
Ditoropo ke tsa mabitso a mose,
Diterata ke tsa mabitso a mose.

A ko shebe feela le masimo a morara!
Motho a ka nahana fela hore o borwa ba Fora.
O ka utlwa ka ona mabitso a boFranschhoek.

Jo! nna, ya tla ya ba ntle Kapa ya ho tuma.
O ko shebe fela matlo a masweu twa!
Tlasa dithaba! ebe a futsitse banga ba o na ka mmala?
Jo! Nna ako shebe fela matlo a motse wa Oranjezigcht!
Ka nnete ha ke so bone bottle botjena!
Utlwang feela mabitso a diterata tsa teng.
Ke boMolteno, Glencoe, Garfield le tse ding.
Tjhe! botle bo tjena hake so ka ke bo bona.

TSELA MOLOI

The Famous Cape

The famous Cape
Cape of the past and present
Cape of tears and sorrow
The Cape of magnificent beauty and goodwill
You distress me as I bring you to mind
You carry countless names
Yet none are that of your own kind
Foreigners have rested on your shore
Sucked blood out of your veins
Gulped water out of your bones
While your greens nurtured them to health

The famous Cape
This nameless name of yours
Is so well known around the world
Your unambiguous mountain is matched up to a table

A label not rightfully yours
They call you a Cape, a Cloth, a Wrap
But who really are you?

Cape you are so admired and unbelievably
You stand bold tall in the world
No wonder why they have taken you away from us
We the children of the Dark Continent
You are where the oceans meet
The seas play outside your back yard
You make those who were sent somewhere to go nowhere

These sailors with their vessels stood unstable at your harbour
I wonder why they didn't fix their ships and moved on?
Even those of Indian decent firmly rested on your chest
And forgot the road back to their motherland
Your councilors awaiting their return
But who can blame them?
Their eyes had set sight upon you
You the land of the Bakgothu people

They should have fixed their boats and travelled on
They should have left the land of the Bakgothu children
Yet they sit and dine around your mountain as if it was a table

Feasted from your crops for years
And in your disbelief they reposed and dispersed
Your wealth among themselves
While there are wide open eyes
Glued upon your San-burnt skinned women
Those beautiful daughters of your lands

There are councilors who could only be in awe of them
These sailors who lusted upon our women
They could only watch as their messengers
Slept and enslaved our dark skinned sisters
Today we know from pre-history
That race was the colour of their tongues
Just like they were blessed with prejudice
Discrimination was imbedded in their blood before 1948
Before they even set foot on our grounds

They raped our mothers in the dark
And children of half blood graced our lands
Yet they walked as if they were better than us
They called themselves gods of knowledge
Saints of true religion
While unbelievably desired daughters of this soil

Indeed your kind has built the famous Cape
Made it look like their front porches of Holland
At times I wonder whose hands and blood built Europe?
Truth be told… Cape is not part of Africa
It does not smell like us
It does not stand like us
Its towns are not named after us
Its streets are not of our people
Look at the grapevine yards!
One would swear he is on the Southern part of France
Who gives a name like Franschhoek?

Oh! How odd and beautiful is the famous Cape
Have you seen how white as snow are its houses?
They look like their foreign owners
Have you heard of Oranjezigcht?
Or taken a walk down Molteno, Glencoe and Garfield street?
Where have you heard of such names?
Indeed these are houses under the shade of our mountain
Seat attractive beyond the imagination
I have never seen such deceiving beautiful beauty.

TSELA MOLOI
Translated by Napo Masheane

Kgibang banana ba Aforika

Kgibang banana ba basetlana kgibang
Kgibang ho re le tle le kgotsofatse boradi-polotiki
    bakontinente
Kgibang ho re batle ba tsebe ho kgotsofatsa mahlo
Mohlomong hona ho tla fetola pelo tsa bona tse kgopo
Kgibang boema fofaneng, meketeng le kae kapakae
Kgibang hore ditau tse tsa dipolotiki di tle di ikgotsofatse
Kgibang ho fihlela tsikinyeho ya mmele wa lona e bakwala
    ditsebe
Tsamaisang ditho tsa lona tsa mmele kaofela
Hore batle ba kgotsofale ka sebele.

Ka nnete kgibang le tiile dithopetsa Aforika
Kgibang mahlo a ditau a bohale a le je abe a le qete
Thothomedisang ditho tsa lona tsa mmele
Mohlomong ho tla ba le kgotso mona kontinenteng

E re ha ntse le kgiba ba le tshware-thware mona le mane
Ka bohlale le ka menwana e kgabisitsweng ka kgauta.
Mohlomong ha ba ntseba ba le tshwara-tshwara
Bokgopo ba bona bo tlaba kokobela
Kapa yona thothomediso ya ditho tsa lona tsa mmele
E tla etsa hore dijo di theohele ha monate ba tle ba tsebe ho
    robala

Boteng ba lona dihukung tsa matlo a bona a majaba-jaba
Bo tla etsa hore banahane hantle mme ka hoo ho rene toka
Kgibang banana ba basetlana
Hore ho tle ho rene kgotso le tswelopele

Kgibang basadi baAforika
Hore le tle le belehe bana ba o e tlabang makgoba a bona
Mohlomong bana ba lona batla tshepahala jwale ka mokgibo
    wa lona
Ha mokgibo wa lona o lokise tse tshwaro e sa nepahalang
Ho bana ba lona e be botaumoholo makgona tsohle

Kgibang le be le kgibisise ditshetlana tsa Aforika ya ho
    tuma.
Kgibang ka mmele ya lona e mesesane
Kgibang ka mmele ya lona e metenya
Kgibang ho fihlela mmele ya lona e kgaoha dikotwana
Thothome tsang dithotsa mmele wa lona hle!
Kgibang basadi ba Aforika e ntle ho fihlela ho ile.

                                TSELA MOLOI

Kgibang Daughters of Africa

Kgibang beautiful daughters of the soil
Kgibang to please these politicians of our continent
Kgibang so that they can have enough for their eyes
This might change their evil hearts
Kgibang at the airport
Kgibang over their extensive meals
Kgibang wherever, whenever

Kgibang beautiful daughters of the soil
Dance and shake your shoulders until their ear drums busts
Twist and turn hard so that they can be fully satisfied
Kgibang like never before daughters of Africa
Dance and shake so that these political vultures can eat you alive
Twist and turn your bodies so that they can see you
They might create peace in our continent

Kgibang beautiful daughters of the soil
Dance so that these monsters can grab your bodies
With their wit and gold wedding rings
May be as they grab your bodies their hearts will soften
Or may be as you boogie and shake hard
They will be able to ingest their food peacefully and sleep well
Who knows, your presence at the corners of their flashy homes
Might make them think about this freedom

Kgibang beautiful daughters of the soil
So that there might be democracy

Kgibang to give birth to imprisoned children of your deeds
They might indeed be more honorable than their fathers
Let your dance moves make all things right
Let your dance moves build great lions pride
Let your dance moves be good medicine to evil

Kgibang beautiful daughters of the African soil
Dance and shake your petite bodies
Dance and shake your voluptuous bodies
Dance and shake all of your body parts
So that these political vultures can fill their appetite
Dance and shake so that the wild beats can enjoy the view
Dance and shake daughters of the soil
Dance until there is no end to your dance moves

TSELA MOLOI
Translated by Napo Masheane

Note: Mokgibo is the most popular female dance-song by Basotho girls. The word derives from the verb ho kgiba (khiba), *which means to perform dance movements with the shoulders while kneeling.*

Remembering the Angolan Bush War
Nervi belli pecunia infinita

He sat in a dust
cracked pan,
hooded eyes,
gnarled hands,
a man who
sewed his soles
back on his feet.

Quick boys!
Just think
of what they
they could do
to us.

Tracer sparked
glowing coals,
slapped, kicked
and danced
while splinters
rained. The
steady rattle,
dreamlike.

There is no
measure of
time. Mute.
Faces pressed
hard into the
sand, as surprise
takes a brutal
stance.

If I suffered what
else could I do.

    GEORGE MOMOGOS

The syncopation of the sounds of your cowhide drum
A tribute to Oswald M Mtshali

The sounds of your cowhide drum
now syncopated with our new world
that for years, remained stretched
as a new skin over my memory has
been woken by its call –
Boom! Boom ! Boom!

The sound leans against a toppled
ideology, holding back the sullied urge
of those deaf to the meandering
message, retrieved by pausing to
hear the sounds of your backbeat –
Boom! Boom! Boom!

As a boy I held my eyes below centre –
I turned away from your cowhide drum
to sounds that were not perpetually possible
for in black and white I've become the
sound that seems to sway. Does today's
passing parade have its eyes below centre?
Boom! Boom! Boom!

GEORGE MOMOGOS

Who are these people?

Ubani lona Mama?
This is your father
From whose seed you were born
You are the blood of his blood
And he loves you
Oh but it hurts when he loves me

Who is this one Mama?
This one is your grandfather
The foundation of your existence
You are his flower
And he cares about you
Mama but his care causes my withering

Lona mama ubani, who is he?
He is your uncle
The pillar of your strength
You are his sunshine
And he is fond of you
But when he fondles me, my world darkens

And who is that man over there, Mama?
Over there is our neighbour
The one who keeps an eye out for us
You are like his own child
And he protects you
I wish someone would protect me from him

Abobani laba Mama, who are these people?
These are the men in your life
The moral custodians of your body and soul
You are their little girl
And they cherish you
Mama these men cause my heart, my body to bleed

Who are these men Mama?
They wound me so deeply
They violate my innocence
They defile my tenderness
Mama these men cause me so much pain

JACKIE MONDI

Khonani ya muduhulu wanga

Khonani ya muḓuhulu wanga wa miṅwaha miṱanu
U nṱalutshedza uri o vhona muḓuhulu wanga
A tshi khou ita zwa vhudzekani
Na kusidzana kwa miṅwaha ya rathi

Kusidzana hoku ndi ṅwana
Wa muhura wanga
Vhana vha khou
Ḓikanzwa nga vhudzekani.

TSHIFHIWA MUKWEVHO

Friend of my nephew

The five-year-old friend of my nephew
Tells me that he's seen my nephew
Having sex
With a six-year-old girl

The girl in question is the child
Of my neighbour:
The kids…
Hey, are enjoying sex.

TSHIFHIWA MUKWEVHO
*Translated by Tshifhiwa Mukwevho
and Gudani Ramikosi*

Ndi humbela maluvha

Ndi humbela maluvha a bvaho mbiluni yanu
Nne uno ndi do a sheledza;
Zwa naka, zwa vha zwavhudi
Lufuno lu simuwaho muyani wanu
Ndi lune nda lila

       TSHIFHIWA MUKWEVHO

Grant me flowers

Grant me flowers from your heart
I will water them
So good it will be, purely pleasant
The love that sprouts from your soul
Is all I need

       TSHIFHIWA MUKWEVHO
       Translated by Tshifhiwa Mukwevho
       and Gudani Ramikosi

Double-jointed Girls

Behind the bicycle shed the older boys
passed around a single joint, while
on the playground, we sat in a circle
and watched the double-jointed girl.
Her skirt tucked into her pants,
she did amazing things with her limbs.
Like a bizarre bird she stood on one leg,
the other pulled up flat against her back.
She manoeuvred her rubbery shoulders
and made us shriek.
She bent her thumbs backwards
to reach her wrists.

I longed to be a double-jointed girl.

Years later, somewhere on a stage,
a troupe of Mongolian girls
with white faces and red lips
flipped backwards on hands and feet
and, with dispassionate eyes,
stared at us through their legs.
Then, like human scorpions,
slowly sidled around in circles.

I thought, so this is what life unfurls
for double-jointed girls.
I thought, perhaps it's just as well
we do not get to choose.
I thought this has been better for me
a single-jointed girl
pulling up,
manoeuvering,
joining
words.

            PAMELA NEWHAM

Third Beach, Port St Johns

Like smoke but cold around us.
Hauling beach trappings and children
we walk into it.
Fog.
No sea although through
the white a sound like waves.

After a while it lifts and we see
shapes, faint at first,
familiar and impossible.
Cows.
Such solid ghosts these.

They watch us with unbaffled eyes
as if we with spades and buckets
and beach towels are out of place.
Cows.
Come to lick the salt.

Later we swim
naked as seals.

PAMELA NEWHAM

A Story Pretending it's a Poem

It rains so quietly here on the farm.
And everyone at the party
is fine about the rain,
sweet about it.

The sun goes down
and cold touches everything.
So everyone hugs the old coal stove
and sits and watches
the 19-year-old shepherd feed it
chopped wood and speak in English,
with a coy smile and
an apology that his English isn't better.
He tells horror stories in English
of why Cape is worse than Jozi
and how he doesn't like gangsters
and never drinks except Smirnoff
and then only on special occasions
'like this one', he says,
and he feeds the fire.

The only white man
points to his black wife
and says how they fooled SA police.
He strokes his beard
and says what it is to long for another;
he climbed walls
and dodged curfews
and, to avoid confusion,
told 'all those white people'

who his wife was just in case
they thought he was one of them.
She, sitting, warms her fingertips;
She lets him talk.

We watch the stove
until party and fire die out.
Goodnights are traded
and I walk with friends to our room.
We, three of us, sleep only after
I read aloud ten pages from a book,
each page I turn I am certain
they will yawn and drift
but they hang on words
egg me to read chapter after chapter.
'Do people still read?' I ask
'Will reading die?'
'No,' they say.
But with no good reason why not.

We sleep.
And day continues on to its own end.

You know, here at the farm
it rains so quietly and so very perfectly.
And after we'd slept
and day continued along
the drunk people from the party came.
Loud and upset with hacking laughs;
opening doors and lights

calling for beds and blankets.
They found mattresses
and cursed the hosts.

One man took one woman
and climbed onto the spring next door.
She squealed and grunted.
He shouted drunken things.

They banged into each other
long and hard towards dawn.
Desperate and hungry,
they startled daylight.

You know, those people,
they woke thunder.

     YEWANDE OMOTOSO

Stranger

sometimes when i'm out shopping
or something i meet my mother.
i'm walking an aisle
and then i turn a corner
and she's there
but doesn't see me.
she's bald and
clutching a bag, like a soldier
carries his rifle;
she's tired but pretending;
she's beautiful
and alone
and she wants to live

YEWANDE OMOTOSO

The Rain

One day
after my mother died
and two years passed
it rained.
We'd collected
All her things
into a pile in the yard
and they got washed away:
the signposts of the past,
the scrap, the spoils.

We had stalled about these things.
We'd thought
put it all out
then walk around;
take our time
and think:
what to remove
what to keep.
We'd thought.

And then it rained
and the rain decided.
You see how little we know.
And even though so much still pains
mostly now we just shrug.

Sometimes it's like that
Sometimes the rains decide.

    YEWANDE OMOTOSO

Robberg

In Plettenberg Bay's summer haze
you beam all-braces through wind-swept hair,
slide into a wetsuit, unaware of your early teen grace.
For the sake of mom-daughter time I squeeze into mine.

Rubber duck skims the waves,
we clutch our seats. Frisky male tourists
grunt when they spot the Mountain of Seals.
Anchor drops like a blue diamond into the deep.

"Watch her please, she's anxious!"
I tell the guide with the shark shield.
Sunrays skim your gleaming shape
as you capsize over the edge, escape…

    I panic and plunge
      follow you down
        down… to white sand

      shoot up for air gulp water –
     waves wash me to sharp rocks
   where seal pups squeal

  and   waddle   to   the   edge –
   They dive… dart around: deep under I find

      curious creatures suspended in space,
        whiskered snouts pressed to your face.

Who's mine, who's pup?! Misted up and up-tight
I resign – join the more relaxed, fin-footed grown-ups.
Further out we float on our backs, scouting the surf for
    great whites.

◐

And that was how, my little seal,
I learnt from moms in furry skins
before you left for boarding school
how letting go begins.

MARÍ PETÉ

Warwick Junction

Down by the crossing he waits for the light –
it turns green. He looks left, then right,
revs to go... but oh, a river of women
(in which he fears he could drown)
wells up towards his yellow bike:

They are not afraid!
Bodies sway in patterned cloth,
bananas bunched on heads,
babies on backs, beaded necks,
cell phone gossip and song.

Johnnyboy says a prayer
before he is flattened
by such sisterhood

but in the nick of time (as if
struck by a kierie) the river parts,
a delta flows around him:

his fear dissolves
in smells of soap,
ginger root, and love
on balmy nights.

Further down where bunny chows are sold,
old apartheid stories told, the stream
snakes round, away…

Johnnyboy blinks,
revs his bike. The light
turns red again.

                        MARÍ PETÉ

Four stages of surgery

I: looking back

the night before i try to locate my life
by offering up a breast – the right –
a sudden recall: how i suddenly
would lift my top to flash my tits
it comes to me now as new as then:
your delight
my pleasure

II: looking down

how it startles me
the nothing, the sudden space
but wait! the something...
                oh.
just the wing of my ribs
beating in its cage of skin
going nowhere

III: seeing straight: mastectomy plus three weeks

Flat now
where once wonder rose
so
flat
that
no outline survives

in eye of mind, memory's home
(though sometimes pads of fingers
like to think they know better)
Across the flatland
this hand unfeeling
untrained
sees new beauty
passing through shadows

IV: following insurrection, resurrection

In the shade cast by silence
resurrection felt its way
reached through my skin
drummed down my blood
and skittled my bones
Then, like a cowboy, it burst out
laughing
and spread daisies in my brain

GILLIAN RENNIE

Spring in New York

As if the buxom tulips weren_it enough,
opening greedily, lapping the sun's juices,
there are the magnolias, on every avenue
wanton buds are crimson with the strain of thickening.
Not to mention the too-close couples who,
too far still from kiss and tell, stay busy on the subway
with kiss and murmur – and that annoying nibbling
they do. All over
Manhattan is in musth. Plus
someone let the elephants out so that
every day there they are, leafing
through parks, turning
up on book covers, dancing
in Union Square, lining
that skirt in the West Side window, arsing
around the platform at West 14th, reminding
me, all of them, along with every vivid petal loosening
itself to die underfoot on the sidewalk,
that this love, ancient and wise and always, failing
– foolishly – to shamble
off to die in some mysterious valley,
measures the beat of my heart.

GILLIAN RENNIE

That Heart

that heart of mine
the one you ripened
until it wanted to burst its skin

that heart
that one split eventually
and from its rent
you sucked its fruit
taking nourishment
plumpness
juicy seeds

you swallowed some of them,
some you kept under your tongue
to take home
far away

maybe you kept them in a jar on a windowsill
so that they would grow more hearts for you
and you could admire them, and say
that heart
that heart
and
that heart
all were hers
but now are mine

GILLIAN RENNIE

The elephant is unhappy

The ground is squelchy underfoot.
The elephant is unhappy.
The grass sparse, wet.
A dog is chained to a table.
"I am on guard," is the sign
around a caravan.
At the next caravan, a woman
holding a cigarette retreats
to its shuttered interior.
The chained dog finds shelter
beneath the camping table,
its tail between its legs.

In the field by the main road
the elephants have attracted onlookers.
A mother holds her child.
The elephants are still, silent.
An elephant blows dust onto herself,
burrowing a hole into the ground
as she sucks up dust, blows it,
uses her trunk to enlarge a hole at her feet.

Her hide is wrinkled grey.
Beyond her cars stream along the wide,
sun-bleached road.
She is tethered by foot,
held by a stake in the ground.
Men sort hay and grass.
The elephant moves, her ears flap,
her trunk grasps into the air,

she sways, the chain stretches, just
before she reaches the end of the chain's pull,
she stops, sways, knows she can't go any further.
Her trunk reaches out again.
Her big body sways slightly,
a foot moves forward. The elephant is unhappy.

Silently, we walk away. The ground is
squelchy underfoot, and the caravans
are inscrutable: you can't see through
their small lace-covered windows.

ARJA SALAFRANCA

i wish i could write

i wish i could write
the way i paint. i paint
the way i eat. there is
a voraciousness in the
schmaltzy oils; something
like greasy mutton gravy
accumulating shape
in wipings of rice. there is
a gorging in the
bristle of brush on clean canvas.
the salacious choosing
of ingredients evaporating
in the drift of cooking steam.
from hand to mouth
i want to write.

but my writing is rather like
deprivation; a blanching
in the wait and wait for the idea
with permission. in the fastidious
weighing between such word
and such. reticently i write –
this and this theme: taboo.
that and that expression:
too sentimental.

i have no wish for my painting –
the searching line is its own satiety.
again and again i find myself here:
my plates and my dishes empty;
and my pages prescriptively full.

        ANDRIES SAMUEL

Untitled

in the week before my daughter left
i became bug-eaten,
bitten in whorls of rash,
mite bites and slashed
with scratches.
i had already acquired
the school-dose of lice
internationally transplanted
to this southern paradise.
but these gnawings
were something else —
unaccountable cusps
of bran and carapace
entangled my wrists
and my ankles. looking
for a skein, a vein
a stigmata.

when she disappeared; my daughter
into the terminal;
i was left winded.
my breath chasing
the stab of spleen
of a runner caught up
by an air, blossoming hornets.

ANDRIES SAMUEL

Rombu Unbu

I say mi amor.

I think I should say
Rombu unbu, but
I do not know the words

so I close my eyes.

I wish for rabbits' whiskers
but his lips grow
a tongue touching

a stitch for unlearnt thuni.

His beard makes
small holes in me,
drawing blood.

Rombu unbu.

Ghost words fill my lips
in a split second that stirs
my mother tongue.

      FRANCINE SIMON

Tamil Familiars

Grandmother used
to warn me not to whistle:
I'd call the snakes.

She forbad me
to sleep with my hair open:
I'd wake up looking like a pichachi,
gone to hell and back.

She said not to eat
out of the pot or it would rain
on my wedding day

I did and I do.

My mother tells me not to
pick from the curry leave tree
when it's that time of month.
Thing will die. She says.

Funny. It hasn't died yet.
And I never give a thought
to my wedding.

     FRANCINE SIMON

Longitude, Latitude

Lines you learnt on the map,
Lines of your house, your nest,
Meridians of your body
Going up and down,
Criss-crossing
In the name of the Father,

Going out, coming in
Their magnetic pull like the moon on the sea,

Lines of attraction, loving,
Lines of fiery animosity,

Lines of writing,
Trying to make sense,

Leylines,
Lines of power that cross the earth,
McGregor, Table Mountain,
To help us to align.

I trace a cross on your forehead,
A kiss on your lips,
A heart on your back.

I draw these lines to help me see.

DEIRDRE SLEMON

An Older Person I Know

He walks with a staggering limp,
Footfalls on wood,
His gait its own rhythm.
Descends the stairs backwards,
Left hand on the rail,
One foot at a time

He learnt to write again
With his left hand,
'spidery' once
after 18 years is cursive, flowing

He learned to speak again,
Finish his sentences, find his words,
Once he said 'Cohen' when he couldn't find 'Jewish'

He learnt to drive again
Bring the dog for walks
Unleashed

He learned to nurse his wife,
Changed the sheets at night,
Railed,
Cooked for her,
Helped her up when she fell

He learned to be alone,
He reads, he meditates,
Grows chilli, spinach, chives
Tomatoes and gives much away

Today he sits with his book and his beer
Watching the sea,
His hair is too long,
I take in the discoloured toenails
And simply ask if his feet are ok,
'No bother. They just swell a bit.'

He says the roses are still blooming
on his wife's anniversary,
and the Pepper tree
she liked refuses to die.

      DEIRDRE SLEMON

Things

Things crowd in
this summer afternoon
of late sunlight
on a gunmetal sea

Things I try to push away,
not wanting them
to crawl and multiply
in this secluded place

Things I cannot allow
to foul my fought-for days
and staked-out solitude,
things that smell of smut

Things that buzz and beat
against the computer screen
wanting out, out, out
reeking of retribution

It rained this morning,
the heat is broken
and so is the spell
I have spun around myself

Unravelled it is, cleft
like a cocoon cut open
exposing my unready heart
to the words on the screen

Look, see, read:
The things said and done
by people to people:
Things I want undone.

   ANNETTE SNYCKERS

Love strays

so unobtrusively and walks across
a prayer mat, gently rubbing fur
against your leg, nibbles your toes
while you supplicate and declare
the demise of matter.

Through the quietude
a warmth touches
feet striding in celestial glow –
you surrender to this love

that binds the Being of all
to a covered heart.

You recall a witness's account
of a Messenger who while paying obeisance
paused to stroke the cat
that interrupted submission.

Immersed in such congruence
& the beneficence of effort
a casual meeting between creatures
simplifies sanctity in these interstices.

                    ABU BAKR SOLOMONS

Another Country

Saturday night
At the police station
And across the road,
The four of us
Making believe
We could not hear –

Beneath our hard
Laughter, our sipping
Wine, our guessing
Games of tunnels
Balloons, strawberries
Beer and spoons –

The screams,
As they lurched
Across the night

Like a drawstring,
Yanked our faces
Tight.

    TANIA SPENCER

Venice, in My Garage

On the floor, against the wall,
I have an olive-green picture of
Venice, in my garage.
The glass is cracked.

He pushes the lawnmower
Past it. Leaves a
Picture, of him
Pushing the lawnmower past
The olive-green picture of
Venice, in my garage.
The glass is cracked.

I keep it like that.
And the floor unswept.
I like to hear the
Gritty roll of lawnmower
Wheels across the floor.

I like to watch the
Greens darken where they
Are caked around the wheels,
Unsweeten to an olive-green,
As he parks it at the back,
Goes inside.

Long after, the sound
Of wheels turning on grit,
Persists. And I am not surprised.
By the traction of dreams
Pulling themselves slowly
Forward over real life.
Like crocodiles, that hope
You will forget about them.

No, I am not surprised.
I keep it like that.

                TANIA SPENCER

What will I put in my box?

I will put in my box
An imaginary island from when I was young
The sound of a blade being unsheathed
The feeling of sand slipping through my fingers.

I will put in my box
A house that moves itself
The yellow sun gently touching the moon
The wag of a puppy dog's tail.

I will put in my box
Two blue teardrops from a dragon
The wet smile of a dolphin
The last dry breath of a desert fox.

I will put in my box
An eleventh commandment and a dry sea
A nun with a gun
And a soldier in a habit.

My box is fashioned from sunken subs,
Sweet silver and sour shade,
With kings crowns on the lid
Gold nuggets in the corners and
Hinges made from the eyelids of angels.

I will use my box to fly through the Universe
To visit an alien race on route to the end of space.
Then wash up in the Milky Way
That feels like sand.

                        LUKE STAMMERS

Bulima nigyeke
Ku JC Dlamini-uBulimangiyeke

Ngokucikoza kwakho ugiya,
Uqephuza kushunq' uthuli;
Ngifisa ukuba ngasemoyeni,
Lezo ntuli zithunqele ngakimi,
Hleze ngihishwe yilobuciko
Nami ngisukume ngicikoze.

Ukube kunembiza okuvutshelwa kuyo
Ukucikoza kwakho
Bokunkondloza njengawe,
Bengoncinda, ngincindile,
Hleze ngihube, ngihashe, ngihaye
Njengawe Bulima ngiyeke!

Ukub' ufuzo luyakhethwa,
Lukhiwa esihlahleni okwamathunduluka,
Ngabe esimila awakho sesabamagatshagatsha.
Ngabe ngisiqapha ngawokhozi imini nobusuku
Ngingafuni namfinyezi ikhalele ngakuso,
Ngigweve naso ngibe yigovu ngigoloze.

Lokhu kudlisela kwakho kokunkondloza
Kungiphendul' elikhulu igovu.
Sengathi ngingagweva,
Ukunyathela kwami kube nguwe,
Nokunyathela kwakho kube yimi.
Kuphele engonyathela ngakho –
Ngibe uBulimangiyeke isibili.

Pho nawe awuzenzanga mtanomuntu,
Yisiphiwo owasamukela kongaphezulu,
Nangaphesheya kwelamathongo,
Ngale kwamagquma akwaMpilo.

Ngikhombise lo muthi
Owagawula kuwo lezi khwili
Zobunkondlo ozibhakuzisa ehawini lakho.
Kuncam' izintombi, izinsizwa zonkana
Zib'isikhomololo zikhexe
Lapho usugiya wena Bulimangiyeke.

Suka! Nom' usungadundubala
Ushone le kwelamathongo.
Uyolokhu uhayile nom' ususithele
Izintuli zokugiya kwakho zilokhu zisixhophile.
Banximf' abanximfayo –
Kulungile Bulimangiyeke!

                    BHEKANI THABEDE

Oh Foolishness leave me alone!
To J. C. Dlamini Bulimangiyeke

You weaving poetry,
Your cyclone writing
Leaves dust on my eyes,
I am asphyxiated
To rise and weave like you.

Cooking pot
To cook words like you
Poetise, tasting muti
Would conjure up glee
Hymns of hymns
Composed for you.
Oh! Foolishness leave me alone.

If you were my lineage,
If I were born of your tree
Heaven's tears
Irrigate that tree
Where no birds will chirp
Orchestrate melodies,
I will drift on...

You're weaving poetry
Your poetry cooked
Makes me a gluttony.
I want to walk like you
Use to do.
Your walking will become me
In that way I will have
No shoes but yours.

I will become you
Foolishness oh! Leave me alone
Your ethereal gift
Comes from beyond
Hills and hillocks.

Show me that tree,
Give me that branch
Of poetry that made your shield
Dazed damsel danced
Lads also enchanted
By your music
Oh! Foolishness leave me alone!

Swallowed by time
Sounds rends our ears still
Your verses echoes on corridors
Of life.
Oh! Foolishness leave me alone!

> BHEKANI THABEDE
> *Translated by Linda Ndlovu*

Dlozi lami unqabe

Lapho imijojantaba yontuluntulu,
Lapho amaklwa nemikhonto,
Lapho izizenze nezimbazo
Ziloliwe zibenyezela kuwubumenyemenye –
Dlozi lami unqabe.

Lapho izintelezi zichelwa ungochelwa,
Lapho amanzi amnyama ephehlisisiwe
Lapho sekuququdwe, kwakhwifwa
Lapho sekugovuzwe, kwancindwa ngakhafulwa
Wena dlozi lami uvele unqabe.

Lapho elami iliba selikhonjiwe
Lapho umgodi sewumbiwe wajula
Lapho sengibaliwe kwabangasekho
Lapho sengixikizwa emabhukwini angapha
Ubovele unqabe dlozi lami.

Lapho umugqa obomvu sewudwetshiwe,
Kwathiwa la akasoze eqe,
Weqa uyobe alibangise le
Kwagoqanyawo,
Phesheya kwethuna.
Wena-ke wenqabe unqabisise dlozi lami.

Lapho izinsuku zami ezingamakhulukhulu
Engazigixabezwa nguSoninini sebezibalile
Bazikhomb' eduze ukuphela
Uma wenqabile uyobe usize mina
Wenqabe ngempela dlozi lami.

Lapho imiklwebhe loseyiklwejwe
Lapho izitshopi sezitshopiwe
Lapho izichitho sezifakiwe ngachithwa
Ngodukanezwe nesipoliyane
Sengizohayiza ebumnyameni ngidukenezwe
Ubonqaba dlozi lami ungavumi.

Lapho sengicushwe ngamalumbo
Onsukumbili namahlung' akwaNgwane
Ngigadlwe ngezulu kuphamban' imibani
Amaphukeshe nompunyumpunyu
Wena dlozi lami ubolokhu unqabile.

Nxa sebethi bathwala ngami
Bengenza umkhovu notikoloshe
Nesimbamgodi soqobo ngoqobo
Wena dlozi ubovele unqabe unqabisise.

Lapho sebengidung' ingqondo
Bengihlanyisa bengenz' isithutha
Bengiphendulel' idlozi elinguwe
Belifulathelise belibhekisa endle nasokhalweni
Ubongisiza impela unqabe dlozi lami.

Laph' izinhlahla ziqheliswa uzisondeze
Ugobise umkhonto wephule izizenze
Kunqamuke izibhobo kufe zindengezi
Kugule umantindane kufe namfakabili
Kukhombise okukhulu kabi ukunqaba dlozi lami
Kunjalo kumele wenqabe dlozi lami.

                      BHEKANI THABEDE

Just Rebuke

Hungry spears
Assegais,
Machetes and axes
Have been horned for me,
Shield me.

Where evil spells have been sprinkled
Best witchcraft prepared,
Shield me.

When I see my grave,
Deep like a gorge,
My name scribbled
On the books of life,
Oh hide me in your palm.

When all boundaries drawn,
Death is waking up, getting ready,
You shall sheath me forth.
My thousand days
Will not desist when
You are my floating angel.

Those scars
Deepened,
Evil spells chanted
Driving me into hysteria
Into wilderness,
Save me.
Save me from wells of witchcraft...

Slummy, dreamy land of goblins,
Tikolosh sent to me,
You shall stop them all...

Oh well I could be foolish
Estranged,
Dislodge,
You will embrace me.
Restore my soul,
My ancestor.

> BHEKANI THABEDE
> *Translated by Linda Ndlovu*

Bread

I see a woman step out of the shadows.
She waits for the traffic lights to change
then hobbles into the road
squints at the sun

she drags her club foot between the idling cars
turns to the drivers behind their windows
touches her open mouth, her empty belly
cups her hands

"he roars his engine   he looks away
she combs her hair   she looks away
they turn to talk   they look away
she mouths *no sorry*   she looks away

"today this lady opens her window and hands me her change
a handful of silvers to warm my pocket
enough to buy a full fresh loaf
the sweet smell of money and bread on my hands

"bread enough to fill my belly
soft bread to break and share
enough bread to keep under my pillow
bread like the loaf of my foot"

                                ELIZABETH TREW

Outsider

Little Owl
you flew out of Helen's dream one night
out of her deepest desire   her passionate house
out of the healing pool
stirred by a dusty angel's wing

You spread your wings in her Camel Yard
she filled with her flock of camels and owls
all facing east to the rising sun,
Helen's creatures she made with Koos
in their place of silver and gold and coloured glass
flashing suns and moons   mirrors to catch the light

Helen   small, strange and grey
shunned   cast out by the sneers of neighbours
jeering at her with Koos, a coloured man

Little Owl
you come from Helen's house,
my pale grey bird turning dark in rain
you sit on my stoep beside your eggs
with your broken ear (which I promise to fix)
and your wings tucked in.
Minerva's owl   bird of poetry
my sentinel
looking out with wide, round eyes
at Lion's Head   facing east.

                    ELIZABETH TREW

Raping Nation

How could the silent be so loud?
Why is this darkness not bright enough?
Why are the cries not heard?
In shards our words lie at our feet
We are living in a raping nation
Daily, it is a news sensation.
Date rape, mate rape, child rape
And there is no escape
From this violent rape
The African women cry
And the little children die.

Why are the cries not heard?
HIV is seeping and creeping everywhere
Please bother yourself and care.
There is no comprehension
Of these demonstrations
We need some explanations
Young girls losing their virginities
Children growing up not knowing their daddies
They are worried about their morals, values and principles
But really don't care about the women's future

The African men don't know their responsibilities
And the women have lost their integrity.
Now who must we blame?
The women with short skirts
Or the men who don't have self-control?

We are living in a raping nation
Why are our cries not heard?

                    SANDISILE TSHABALALA

Eybers

Ryg deur die
fyne tasters van jou oë,
soekende en glad –
gelouterde gedagtes vir die hart

ek's verwonderd –
woord-heldin,
oor jou kalme broosheid
die egtheid van jou diep besin

                TOBIE VERMAAK

Eybers

Thread through the
Delicate probes of your eyes,
seeking and smooth –
purified thoughts for the heart

I'm amazed –
word-heroine,
by your calm frailty
the authenticity of your deep reflection

                TOBIE VERMAAK
Translated by Johann de Lange

Liefdestaal

Jy klee my in die liefde –
'n sagte woord, 'n blik

die streling van jou skrale hand
vertel die ou-ou mooi verhaal

'n liefdestaal vloei uit jou wese
in die vreugde van jou vroulikheid

mý taal gaan in woorde uit
en sing met jou 'n hooglied saam

                TOBIE VERMAAK

Language of love

You clothe me in love –
a soft word, a look

the caress of your slender hand
tells the old, old beautiful story

a language of love flows from your being
in the joy of your femininity

my language goes forth in words
singing a song of songs with you

                TOBIE VERMAAK
          Translated by Johann de Lange

Wildtuin-huisie

Kom ons vra en bou 'n huisie
van klip en glas en óóp
'n wye stoep –
hoor jy die byevanger roep?

ons bou dit by Sereni
in die noordebos,
waar patryse roep in hul histerie
en olifant besoekbewyse los

met jakkalsbessie, rooiwilg
en mopanie
as bure, stilles ook
hul vra nie eintlik vrae nie

ons vier die dagbreek, elke more
en prys die Heer –
dat Hy oor al dié mooiste dinge
in heerlikheid regeer!

    TOBIE VERMAAK

Game park-hut

Let's ask and build a hut
of stone and glass and open
a wide veranda –
can you hear the bee-pirate calling?

we build it at Sereni
in the northern bush,
where partridges call hysterically
and elephants leave calling cards

with jakkalsbessie, red-willow
and mopani
for neighbours, quiet too
they don't really ask questions

we celebrate daybreak, every morning
and praise the Lord –
that He rules over all these beautiful things
in splendour!

TOBIE VERMAAK
Translated by Johann de Lange

Biographies

Saleeha Bamjee
Bamjee is an editorial consultant and photographer based in Johannesburg. She is learning how to read and write through Rhodes University's MA Creative Writing programme. She blogs at www.saaleha.com.

Brett Beiles
Beiles was born in Johannesburg, raised in Durban, but grew up in Europe and the UK. He returned to South Africa due to ill health, and now has his mental health tested as a copywriter in an ad agency. He adjudicated festivals for the SA Speech & Drama Association, which further tests his mental stability. He has also worked in circus, theatre, journalism and car parks. Several of his poems and short fiction have been published in anthologies and journals in SA and abroad, and he has won a few prizes for his work, as well as judged in some poetry competitions. For six years Beiles was governor of the Lives of Poets Society (LiPS) in Durban (founded in 1995 and still going strong).

Michele Betty
Betty grew up in Johannesburg, Gauteng, and was schooled at St Theresa's Convent in Rosebank. She enrolled to read for a Bachelor of Arts at the University of the Witwatersrand, majoring in Psychology and Law, which she completed in 1993. Thereafter, she read for a Bachelor of Law degree which she completed in 1995. She serviced articles at Brugmans Incorporated, a law firm which specialised in insurance litigation, and was admitted as an attorney in

1997. She took up employment at Investec Bank Limited, where she gained a solid commercial background. Thereafter, she moved to Webber Wentel Bowen's commercial law department, where she specialised in mergers and acquisitions. Michele is married and has two children. She and her family relocated to Cape Town in 2008.

Vonani Bila
Bila was born in 1972 in Elm/Shirley village in Limpopo province. He runs the Timbila Poetry Project in Limpopo, which holds poetry workshops, organises exchange programmes and readings, and publishes the groundbreaking *Timbila Poetry Journal* as well as individual collections of poetry. He is the author of eight storybooks in English, Northern Sotho and Xitsonga for newly literate adult readers. His poetry books include *No Free Sleeping* (with Alan Findlay and Donald Parenzee), *Throbbing Ink*, *In the Name of Amandla* and *Magicstan Fires*, including poems written mostly at the PEN Belgium Dutch Writers' flat in Antwerp, Belgium, where Bila spent July 2004 as a resident poet. His recent collection, *Handsome Jita*, was published by the UKZN Press in 2007. Bila has read poetry in South Africa, Brazil, Sweden, The Netherlands, Ethiopia, Ghana, Finland, Algeria and Indonesia. Some of his best poems have been translated into French, Arabic, Turkish, Finnish, Indonesian Bahasa, Swedish and Dutch. Bila is currently doing an MA in Creative Writing at Rhodes University.

Drees Claasen
Claasen is a Theatre and Performance student at the University of Cape Town with a passion for reading and writing. A tweny-one-year-old guy from South Africa, when he's not writing he's pretending to be an actor; his motto is: take your future one day at a... Since his school days he's been an active participant on poetry websites with some success in getting positive comments on his efforts.

Christine Coates
Coates has an MA in Creative Writing from the University of Cape Town and is a writer and writing coach. Her stories and poems have been published in various literary journals. Her poems have been published in *New Coin*, *New Contrast*, *Carapace*, *A Hudson Review* and other literary journals. Two poems were selected for the inaugural *Sol Plaatje European Union Poetry Anthology* in 2011. Her poem *Found Poem* was a finalist in the Cambridge Conference of Contemporary Poetry Review 2002, Africa Focus.

Tanita da Silva
Da Silva loves writing, especially in her mother tongue. Her belief is that words are magic, or rather "mens kan toor met woorde". She is a teacher of mathematics and dramatic arts. She also does freelance writing for various newspapers (*Die Burger*, *Tuinroete* en *George Herald*) and a magazine (*Kuier-tydskrif*). Some of her articles were published in the *Sondagson*. Additionally she was a correspondent for *KaapRapport* until November 2011. Tanita is married and has two children.

Gail Dendy

Dendy's first collection of poetry, entitled *Assault and the Moth*, was published by Gerville Press in 1993. This was followed by *People Crossing* (Snailpress, 1995), *Swimming in the Long Dark Sound* (Stride, 1998), *Painting the Bamboo Tree* (Arc, 1999), *The Poetry of Norman Corwin and Gail Dendy* (Shirim, 2002) and *The Lady Missionary* (Snailpress, 2007). Her seventh collection, *Closer than That*, was published by Dye Hard Press in 2011). Gail, originally from Durban, is married and now lives in Johannesburg. Over the years she has worked, inter alia, as a university lecturer, copywriter and radio news writer. She is currently the library and research specialist for an international corporate law firm.

Julian de Wette

De Wette was born in Cape Town in 1951. He attended South Peninsula High School in Diep River (where he was privileged to be taught by the writer and scholar, Richard Rive). He is a graduate of Sarah Lawrence College in Bronxville, New York, where his don was the novelist, Edgar Doctorow. In May 2011, De Wette was invited to participate in the Franschhoek Literary Festival. Last year his play, *Sister Priscilla's Dilemma: The Nun With a Gun*, was selected as one of the top five plays from South Africa for the Theatre in Translation initiative run by Proyecto 34°S in Buenos Aires. He has been invited to attend a staged reading of the Spanish version of *Sister Priscilla* in Buenos Aires later this year.

Graham Dukas

Dukas was born in Cape Town in 1954. He has lived in various parts of the Western Cape but is happy to call Cape Town his home. He studied architecture at the University of Cape Town in the '70s and early '80s. He no longer practises as an architect but is a part-time member of the academic staff at the University's School of Architecture. His professional time, though, is spent as a facilitator, mentor and coach where he helps in the growth and development of business leaders.

Sarah Frost is thirty-eight years old and a single mother to an eight-year-old boy. She works as an editor for *Juta Legalbrief* in Durban, South Africa. She has been writing poetry for the past fourteen years. She has completed an MA in English Literature, and also a module on Creative Writing through the University of KwaZulu-Natal. She has published in various SA journals and also some in the US. Frost's first anthology, *Conduit*, was published by Modjaji Books in the first quarter of 2011.

Genna Gardini

Gardini is a writer based in Cape Town. Her poetry has been published in various national and international literary journals, including *Carapace*, *Itch*, *New Coin*, *New Contrast*, *African Writing* and *The Common*. Her poems appear in the 2007 *POWA Breaking the Silence: Murmurs of the Girl in Me* and 2011 *Mapping Me* anthologies. She was chosen as one of Art South Africa's Bright Young Things for 2009 and was a featured poet on the Badilisha Poetry Radio in 2010. In 2011, Gardini was featured as a commended poet in that year's *Aesthetica Creative Works Annual* and, later that year, was longlisted for the 2011 *Sol Plaatje European Union*

Poetry Award. In 2012, some of her poetry was included in the group exhibitions Sometimes: An Exhibition of Texts (Cape Town) and The Problem with International Relations: A Collection of Love Letters (London). Since early 2012, she has written a quarterly column for *Itch* on young South African poets. Gardini also works as an arts journalist and scriptwriter. She is currently completing her Honours in Drama at UCT.

Dawn Garisch
Garisch has had five novels and a collection of poetry published, a short play and short film produced, and has written for television, magazines and newspapers. Three of her novels have been published in the UK. In 2010 *Trespass* was shortlisted for the Commonwealth Prize in Africa, and in 2011 her poem *Miracle* won the EU Sol Plaatje Award. A non-fiction work, *Eloquent Body*, is out, published by Modjaji books. She runs workshops on writing and creative method, is a practising medical doctor and lives in Cape Town. She currently is working on a memoir about dance.

Anthea Garman
Garman teaches writing and editing to journalism students in the School of Journalism and Media Studies at Rhodes University, where she is an associate professor. She also teaches Media Studies to "first years" and supervises Master's and Doctoral degrees. She edits the publication *Rhodes Journalism Review*. Garman has been writing poetry steadily since a teenager. She has a husband who is a superb cook and designer, a 21-year-old daughter studying Fine Art, and two rambunctious Staffordshire terriers who consume energy and time and who she tries desperately to convert to the techniques of the Dog Whisperer. She lives in Grahamstown.

Dorian Haarhoff

Haarhoff is a poet, story-teller, and children's writer who runs creative writing and story-telling workshops. He believes in the ability of people to revitalise their workplace, build their communities, participate in their healing and find their joy. Dorian is a former professor of English at the University of Namibia, and has also taught in the Canadian Creative Writing Faculty. Since 1998, he has run his own business, Creative Workshops. Dorian has thrice been invited as poet and as a guest story-teller to the Conference of Word Affairs in Boulder, Colorado. He was a participating poet at Poetry Africa Durban 2004 and at the International Poetry Festival in Colombia, South America, 2005. He lives in Somerset West.

Joan Hambridge

Novelist and poet, literary critic and academic, Hambridge teaches Afrikaans Literature and Creative Writing at the University of Cape Town. A prolific and multi-faceted author and reviewer, she holds a PhD from Rhodes University and from the University of Cape Town. Her poetry has been widely published internationally and she won the Eugéne Marais Prize for Literature and the Litera Prize. Her latest volume of poems is *Lot se vrou* and she has several satirical and non-satirical novels to her name, including *Die Judaskus*, *Palindroom* and *Kladboek*.

Kerry Hammerton

Hammerton is a poet, writer and alternative health practitioner. Her poetry has been published in South African literary journals *Carapace*, *New Contrast* and *New Coin*, online at Litnet, Incwadi and Slipnet. Her work has also been published overseas in *Magma Poetry*. Some of her poems were included in the anthology *Difficult to Explain* (Finuala Dowling ed. Hands on Books, 2010). *These are the Lies I told You*, her first poetry collection, was published by Modjaji Books in 2010.

Geoffrey Haresnape

Haresnape was born in Durban and brought up in Cape Town. He is a poet and writer of fiction with five volumes of poetry published to date: *Drive of the Tide* (1976), *New-Born Images* (1991), *Mulberries in Autumn* (1996), The *Living and the Dead: Selected and New Poems* (2005) and *Where the Wind Wills* (2011). He has a prize-winning novel *Testimony* (1991) and a collection of short stories, *African Tales from Shakespeare* (1999). He is Emeritus Professor of English at UCT.

Siddiq Khan

Khan lives in Cape Town, South Africa, where he was born at 8pm during a shrill April evening in the year 1990. A product of his times, his time's been spent within the murderously narrow ranges of passions, adventures, threats and opportunities presented to him by his society, of whom he is an irreconcilable enemy. His action is both a result and (all too partial) negation of his thoroughly dissatisfying situation. He is a worker engaged in precarious labour, an editor of *Love Letters Journal*, an online publication of revolutionary theory, an amateur astronomer, a film-maker, an enthusiastic gardener, as well as an initiator of various half-baked subversive schemes currently languishing in a state of suspended animation.

Kobie Korf

Korf currently runs a small business on labour issues in Durban. He worked as a nutritional advisor after completing a diploma in nutrition. His real calling, however, was that of a librarian, and he worked as one in Mpumalanga and Limpopo for many years. Most of all, he would like to be a 'word-farmer'. He writes poetry and has had some of his poems published on the internet. Last year he had published *The Heart of Nelson Mandela*, his epic tale. The SABC then recorded the CD with voice artists, the Durban's Men's Choir and Mandela himself. It was done in Afrikaans and English.

John Kruger

Kruger is a seventy-six-year-old pensioner living in Goedemoed, Durbanville in the Western Cape. He was a high-school principal for twenty-one years – eight years at Vryburg High and thirteen years at Worcester High. He obtained a BA degree with Afrikaans-Netherlands and Psychology as main subjects, as well as a UOD diploma from the University of South Africa. He also received an Honours Diploma in bookkeeping and accounts from the College of Accountancy. His hobbies are writing and painting.

David Maahlamela

Maahlamela is an award-winning poet and prose writer who hails from Mankweng in Polokwane, Limpopo. Writing mainly in Sepedi and English, Maahlamela's work has featured regularly for over a decade in literary journals and anthologies such as *New Coin*, *Timbila*, *Carapace*, *Botsotso*, *New Contrast*, *Kotaz*, *Fidelities*, *English Academy Review*, *Echoes*, *Green Dragon*, *Turfwrite*, *Magic with Words*, *Itch*,

Amandla, *So much to Tell*, *There is a Place* and *The Edge of Things*. Maahlamela has performed in various events such as the South African Literary Awards, Anglo Platinum Limpopo Achiever Awards, Northern Cape Writers Festival, Polokwane Book Fair, Jozi Book Fair, Cape Town Literary conference, Free State Library Celebration, Durban Verses for Biko, Mpumalanga 16 Days of Activism, Zimbabwe Solidarity Rally Poetry Africa and the Washington DC ISP convention.

Chris Mann
Mann is based at the Institute for the Study of English in Africa in Grahamstown. He is the honorary professor of poetry at Rhodes University. His other work experience includes being an English teacher at a rural school, a junior lecturer in the Department of English at Rhodes University, founder and chair of the Teacher Development Foundation, a trustee of the Donaldson Trust, a member for five years of the Rhodes Scholarship selection committee in KwaZulu-Natal, co-founder and song-writer of Zabalaza, a cross-culture band performing in English and Zulu (winner of the SATV Follow-that-Star new band competition), a member of the National Economic Forum's Task Team on job creation, a parish councillor, Deputy CEO of the Grahamstown Foundation, secretary of Spiritfest and co-founder of the Masikhulisane Trust. His language competence, at different levels, includes Zulu, Afrikaans, Xhosa and Italian. He and the artist Julia Skeen were married in 1981. They have two children and live in Grahamstown.

Michelle McGrane

Born in 1974 in Zimbabwe, McGrane spent her childhood in Malawi and moved to South Africa with her family when she was fourteen. She has lived in Johannesburg since 2007. Her recent collection, *The Suitable Girl*, is published by Pindrop Press in the United Kingdom and Modjaji Books in South Africa. Her work deals with societal expectations, gender, death, grief and mythology, and looks at how women, historical or actual, have "shaped their interior landscapes and, in doing so, shaped the world". "[Her] poems refuse to lie down in the boxes set out by history or society. Instead, they describe women who are complex, difficult and pleasingly unsuitable". She is a member of SA PEN and blogs at Peony Moon.

Mari Mocke

Mocke (née Doubell) was born in Tarkastad, lived in Port Elizabeth, where she matriculated from Pearson High School and later relocated to Table View, Cape Town. Poetry and the theatre drive her passion. Her poems have appeared in *Tydskrif vir Letterkunde*, *Contrast* and *New Contrast*, as well as in the children's anthology *Rymreise*. She never goes to bed without first reading a poem or two from an anthology.

Doreen Mojapelo

Mojapelo is a twenty-two-year-old Language and Translation Studies graduate who passed her degree with 14 distinctions. She hails from Ga-Molepo village in the Limpopo province. She mainly writes in English and Sepedi. Doreen is currently studying for an Honours degree in Northern Sotho.

Tsela Moloi

Moloi started writing poetry while he was in exile in Tanzania and Bulgaria from 1978 to 1991. These were tough times during which he longed for his family and his country, and had to focus on his involvement in the struggle for the liberation of his people in South Africa. When he returned to South Africa, he continued writing and being inspired by the new challenges which were faced by the majority of South Africans. This was the time of the last kicks of a dying horse and after the liberation movements were unbanned. Apart from the political topics he has written on, he reflects on socio-economic issues such as poverty, culture and the challenges faced, especially by South Africa's youth.

George Momogos

Momogos lives with his wife Anne and daughter Michelle in Durban, KwaZulu-Natal on the east coast of South Africa, an area framed in the east by the Indian Ocean and in the west by the beautiful Ukhahlamba-Drakensberg mountains. Momogos is a fledgling poet and short-story writer who is busy plotting out a literary course, a marketing and business-strategy expert and an entrepreneur, designing and developing web-based solutions to help organisations implement effective learning programmes. He is adept at formulating and implementing growth and retention for businesses plagued by constitutional change and fluctuating market conditions.

Jackie Mondi

Mondi is a black South African woman, who is a writer, poet and AIDS activist. She is fascinated by the power of the written word and strives to harness this power to change people's lives. Her writing has been published in a number of publications, including *The 2011 Sol Plaatje European Union Poetry Anthology*, *Face the Spirit: Illuminating a century of essays by South African women*, *So Much to Tell Vol. 2: An anthology of South African women writing* and *The South African Labour Bulletin*. Mondi lives in Johannesburg with her husband Lumkile and son Vuyo.

Tshifhiwa Mukwevho

Mukwevho, young writer-cum-poet and human-interest news correspondent, has authored a collection of short stories titled *A Traumatic Revenge* (Timbila, 2011). He has had poems and short stories published in numerous SA literary journals such as *Carapace*, *Botsotso* 14, *New Contrast*, *Timbila*, *Fidelities* and *Makoya* while he was doing time in prison. His crimes were numerous charges of breaking into and stealing from shops in Louis Trichardt, between the age of 12 and 14. He was only released in November 2010. He was born in 1984. While still in prison, Mukwevho was afforded strong support from arts organisations or projects who noticed his writing talent, and therefore motivated him to continue to read and write.

Pamela Newham

Newham moved from Johannesburg to the Cape twelve years ago and now lives in Hout Bay. She began her career as an English teacher before becoming a magazine journalist and features editor. In the past few years, she has turned her attention to fiction writing. In 2010 her first book, *Three Blind Dates* (for girls between the ages of nine and twelve), was runner-up in Maskew Miller Longman's Literature Awards. She has had various short stories published and her poems have appeared in online poetry blogs, *Carapace*,

The Ground's Ear and *Difficult to Explain*, an anthology edited by Finuala Dowling.

Yewande Omotoso
Omotoso was born in Barbados in 1980 and grew up in Nigeria with her parents and two older brothers. The family moved to South Africa in 1992. Yewande trained as an architect at the University of Cape Town, after which she completed a Master's degree in Creative Writing. Her debut novel *Bom Boy* was published by Modjaji Books in 2011 and was shortlisted for the 2012 *Sunday Times* Literary Awards.

Marí Peté
Peté was born in Middleburg and schooled in Witbank (now Emalahleni) in the Mpumalanga province. She studied at the University of Pretoria and the University of KwaZulu-Natal. She holds an Honours degree in Afrikaans and Dutch Literature and a Master's degree in Computer Assisted Education. She has worked as an e-learning specialist at the Durban University of Technology since 1994. Prior to this, she worked at the Faculty of Modern and Medieval languages at the University of Cambridge, England. Peté has published two collections of poetry with Umsinsi Press, namely *Amytis* (1997) and *Begin* (2002). She lives in Durban with her husband Stephen and teenage daughter Megan.

Gillian Rennie
Rennie teaches writing and editing at the School of Journalism and Media Studies at Rhodes University. Before that she worked for a long time in a variety of print media. She has edited *Cue*, the daily newspaper of the

National Arts Festival since 1999, and was a USC Anneberg/Getty Arts Journalism Fellow in 2010. Her profile of MaMbeki in *Fairlady* won a Modi Award for profile writing. She believes polka dots have the power to deliver joy, that starlight is a health drink and – setting aside their disregard for semicolons – that cats know everything.

Arja Salafranca
Salafranca was born in Spain to a Spanish father and South African mother, and has lived in South Africa since the age of five. She received a BA degree in African Literature and Psychology at the University of the Witwatersrand in 1993, and has recently completed her MA in Creative Writing. Her first poetry collection, *A Life Stripped of Illusion* received the 1994 Sanlam Award for poetry, and was followed by a second collection *The Fire in which We Burn*, published in 2000. Salafranca has worked for various newspapers in Johannesburg and now edits the *Life* supplement in the Johannesburg-based national newspaper *The Sunday Independent*.

Andries Samuel
Samuel grew up in the Free State where he won several prizes for poetry and prose as a high-school learner at Grey College. He received a BA degree in Architecture as well as a postgraduate B.Arch. degree at the University of Cape Town. He worked in Tel Aviv and New York between his degrees and currently lives and works in Cape Town. He teaches part-time at the UCT School of Architecture. He works part-time as a writer and translator. His work appears in *New Contrast* and online at Litnet and Versindaba. His debut collection of poetry, *Wanpraktyk*, was published by Human & Rousseau in February 2011.

Francine Simon

Simon was born in March 1990; the firstborn to Roman Catholic parents. She grew up in Morningside, Durban. She began writing poetry around the age of fifteen during her time at Durban Girls' High School. She is currently completing a degree in English Honours at the University of KwaZulu-Natal. Books (whether fiction of non-fiction) have been her passion since a very young age. Literature has had the biggest influence on her as a writer; her main literary influences being Yvonne Vera, Ingrid Jonker, Kobus Moolman, Sylvia Plath and Tea Obreht. Her writing has been described as delicately sobre, surreal and enigmatic. She plans to continue her studies with a Creative Writing Master's in Poetry.

Deirdre Slemon

Slemon was born in Ireland in 1964, but immigrated to South Africa with her family in 1976. She studied languages at the University of Cape Town and did a TFL course at the Institute Brittannique de Paris, as well as completing an MPhil in Applied Linguistics and Language at the University of the Western Cape. She has been a freelance journalist in the arts, doing translation, interpretation and voiceovers in English and French, and currently teaches both languages at Bishops.

Annette Snyckers

Snyckers is a visual artist and poet living in Cape Town. She studied English, French and German at the University of Pretoria and later Fine Art at UNISA. She was a high-school teacher and translator before dedicating herself to the visual arts. She is a painter and an enthusiastic amateur photographer. She lived in Switzerland for three years and has travelled extensively. Every few years she spends three months in Paris in an artistic residency programme. As a lover of language and literature, Annette has always written – either for academic purposes or for pleasure; but in 2010 she started sharing her work at poetry workshops. Some of her poems were published in *Difficult to Explain* edited by Finuala Dowling, in Incwadi and SLiP.

Abu Bakr Solomons
Solomons was born in District 6, Cape Town, and has taught English for some thirty years. He is currently the principal of Spes Bona High School, Athlone. He completed studies in English, Psychology and History at the University of Cape Town, the University of the Western Cape and UNISA. In 1985 he was awarded a Fullbright Scholarship to complete a diploma in TESOL at the University of Iowa. In 1986 he completed a dissertation on the poetry of the South African Arthur Kenneth Nortje for a Master's degree. In 1992 he was awarded a fellowship to pursue the works of Bessie Head, Alex La Guma and Dennis Brutus at the Northwestern University of Chicago. In 1993, whilst being the regional Chairperson of the Congress of South African Writers (COSAW) in the Western Cape, he was selected to participate in the Salzburg Seminar in Austria. His poems have been published in various journals, in a recent anthology published by Botsotso, and in the inaugural *Sol Plaatje European Union Poetry Anthology* of 2011.

Tania Spencer
Spencer is a writer, philosopher, sporadic cartoonist and traveller. She studied social anthropology and philosophy at the University of Natal, Durban. She worked as a journalist on the *Natal Witness* newspaper and later wrote for the

University's stable of in-house publications in Pietermaritzburg. In the '90s she undertook a social documentary photographic project about and with street children in four South African cities (Pietermaritzburg, Durban, Johannesburg and Cape Town). In 2004 she documented, photographically, Japanese tourists' experiences in a small Canadian town, Yellowknife, in the Northwest Territories. Both these projects resulted in solo exhibitions, the former at the Tatham Art Gallery, Pietermaritzburg. She has had various poems and short stories featured in South African publications, including *New Coin* and *Agenda*. In 1985 she was awarded first prize in the *Forge* poetry award by the late Douglas Livingstone.

Luke Stammers
Stammers is a thirteen-year-old boy who currently attends Rondebosch Boys' High school. His poem *What Will I put in My Box*, has been commented on by Finuala Dowling as being "mature and technically way beyond his age group..." He loves rugby, reading, Playstation and pets. He is the son of *Leadership* magazine editor Robbie Stammers.

Bhekani Thabede
Thabede is from Phongola in KwaZulu-Natal but currently resides in Richards Bay where he runs Khula Arts Centre, a self-established arts institution that services artists from UThungulu District in music, dance, visual arts and theatre. He is a writer, producer and director for theatre shows and a researcher for documentaries and films. He is a published author and co-author of literature works prescribed for school in Zulu. He is married to Dollana Thabede who is also a writer.

Elizabeth Trew

Trew born in Cape Town, returned to South Africa in 1991 after 27 years away in England where she was involved in adult education and taught English as an additional language to immigrants and refugees. Back home she continued to teach, and obtained a Master's degree in English Education from the University of the Witwatersrand. She became a volunteer counsellor at People Opposed to Women Abuse (POWA) and continues to serve as a co-ordinator of POWA's women's writing project. Now retired from teaching, she helps at Siviwe and girls' shelters in Cape Town. She is published in many literary journals and poetry magazines and anthologies in both England and South Africa.

Sandisile Tshabalala

Tshabalala was born in 1996 in Pietermaritzburg and currently attends St Francis College. Her interest in poetry started at the age of twelve, and she began writing poems a year later. She enjoys writing multilingual poetry, mixing English, Zulu and Afrikaans.

Tobie Vermaak

Vermaak grew up under the influence of writers like Van Wyk Louw, Eybers and Opperman. He has written short stories and poetry for his own expression and enjoyment for many years, and plans to publish some recent work soon. Professionally, he practised as a management consultant, specialising in the field of business competitiveness. His book *How to become and remain a competitive business* has relevance here. He is a nature lover and spends his free time in the Kruger Park and the southern Cape, studying trees in particular. Another interest is playing duplicate bridge, where he also contributes to the development of bidding techniques.

What is the European Union?

The European Union is a unique economic and political partnership between 27 European countries* that has delivered half a century of peace, stability, and prosperity, helped raise living standards, launched a single European currency, and is progressively building a single Europe-wide market in which people, goods, services and capital move among Member States as freely as within a country.

Created in the aftermath of the Second World War, the first steps taken towards a union were to foster economic cooperation. Since then, the union has developed into a huge single market. What began as a purely economic union has evolved into an organisation spanning all areas, from development aid to environmental policy.

The EU actively promotes human rights and democracy and has the most ambitious emission reduction targets for fighting climate change in the world. Thanks to the abolition of border controls between EU countries, it is now possible for people to travel freely within most of the EU.

How does it work?

European Union countries have set up institutions to run the European Union and adopt its legislation. The main ones are:
- European Parliament (representing the people of Europe)
- Council of the European Union (representing national governments)
- European Commission (representing the common EU interest)

Size and population
At 4 million km² the European Union is roughly one seventh the size of Africa and just over three times the size of South Africa. France is the EU's largest country and Malta its smallest. The EU has a population of close to 500 million people – the world's third largest after China and India.

European Union symbols
- The European flag – the 12 stars in a circle symbolise the ideals of unity, solidarity and harmony among the peoples of Europe.
- The European anthem – the melody used to symbolise the EU comes from Ludwig Van Beethoven's 9th Symphony composed in 1823.
- Europe Day – the ideas behind the European Union were first put forward on 9 May 1950 by French foreign minister Robert Schuman. This is why 9 May is celebrated as a key date for the EU.
- The EU motto – "United in diversity".

The European Union and South Africa – a Partnership of Equals
The growing relationship between South Africa and the European Union since 1994 has been underpinned by the Trade, Development and Cooperation Agreement (TDCA). Closer ties between the two parties were consolidated in 2007 with the establishment of the EU–SA Strategic Partnership.

This partnership, the only one of its kind with an African partner, is centered on enhanced political dialogue around issues of shared interest including climate change, the global economy, governance, bilateral trade, and peace and security matters. In line with this, its action plan encompasses sectoral cooperation on a range of issues such as climate change, environment, education, science and technology, space, trade, migration, etc.

Annual summits and ministerial and senior officials' meetings steer the partnership along with the EU–South Africa Joint Cooperation Council. They provide the occasions to discuss current bilateral, regional and global issues.

Trade cooperation

The European Union remained South Africa's number one trading partner in 2011, accounting for 26% of the value of total SA trade flows. The EU is the most important destination for local exports, accounting for just over 22% of total exports from South Africa. Similarly, the EU remains the biggest source of SA imports at some 31% of total imports.

Development cooperation

The European Union is South Africa's most important development partner by far, providing close to 70% of all external assistance funds. The total indicative budget for the period 2007–13 amounts to €980 million, the largest bilateral envelope worldwide. The EU, its Member States and the European Investment Bank (EIB) annually invest in South Africa over €500 million in grants and loans.

More information can be found at http://eeas.europa.eu/south_africa/

* Belgium, Bulgaria, Czech Republic, Denmark, Germany, Estonia, Ireland, Greece, Spain, France, Italy, Cyprus, Latvia, Lithuania, Luxembourg, Hungary, Malta, the Netherlands, Austria, Poland, Portugal, Romania, Slovenia, Slovakia, Finland, Sweden, and the United Kingdom.